WITH A MEASURE OF GRACE

The Story and Recipes of a Small Town Restaurant

By BLAKE SPALDING and JENNIFER CASTLE

with Lavinia Spalding

Foreword by Terry Tempest Williams

Photographs by Eric Swanson

Designed by Maria Hwang Levy
Photography © Eric Swanson
All recipes © Blake Spalding and Jennifer Castle
Published by Provecho Press, Santa Fe, New Mexico
Printed in Singapore
Fifth edition

Library of Congress Cataloging-in-Publication Data
ISBN 978-0-9719364-2-3

hellsbackbonegrill.com
provechopress.com
hellsbackbonegrill@color-country.net
435-335-7464 restaurant
435-335-7461 fax

MIX
Paper from
responsible sources
FSC® C019704
www.fsc.org

THIS BOOK IS DEDICATED TO THE RESIDENTS OF BOULDER TOWN.

MAY THEY AND ALL BEINGS HAVE PERFECT HAPPINESS.

Table of Contents

Prayer Flags in the Desert

BY TERRY TEMPEST WILLIAMS

It was with some trepidation that I left the town of Torrey and drove down Highway 12, heading toward Boulder for a gathering of the Southern Utah Wilderness Alliance. I realized that I hadn't been in Garfield County since the spring of 1997, when the Grand Staircase-Escalante National Monument was less than a year old. Back then, the town seemed raw—the new monument yet another insult threatening their unabashed frontier lifestyle. Most residents made themselves emotionally off limits to outsiders visiting the wild and vast area, now federally protected. The rest were plain mad and not hesitant to show it— dark glares beneath sweat-stained ball caps; curtly spoken, few-worded answers to innocent questions; one-dimensional exchanges in convenience stores (no conversation, no eye contact, only money moving, hand to hand). The air was cold and thick with unspoken resentments.

Locals saw no need for more protection of the landscape they'd assumed was theirs since Brigham Young sent their ancestors down to spread his gospel. Why protect godforsaken land that had done a fairly good job of protecting itself? They saw the new monument only from the perspective of rural economics—any additional protection would attract more people, making a difficult living more so. Tourists were a nuisance and a distraction from the real work of real people.

But not everyone feels this way. The red hot sandstone is a magnet for passionate engagement, a sensual landscape that inspires love—a wild terrain to be explored and respected.

For decades, people from all over the United States have become involved in efforts to protect Utah's redrock wilderness. The Escalante canyons are at the heart of this proposal. America's Redrock Wilderness Act is now a bill before Congress, with hundreds of cosponsors in the House of Representatives and dozens of sponsors committed in the Senate, all of whom acknowledge the rarity of this landscape of the imagination. Redrocks and ravens, serpentine canyons, and maidenhair ferns that decorate water-drenched grottoes seep into our DNA. We are changed on a cellular level and begin to see the world differently. We remember why the desert is holy, a place for pilgrims in search of peace. We touch stone and find an opening. Erosion of rock inspires an erosion of our own calcified nature.

I was nervous to return to Boulder. The last time I was there someone threw a rock at my car. I didn't understand until later, when I realized I had a "Wild Utah" sticker on my rear bumper.

Coming from rural Mormon stock myself, I understood the grittiness, the calluses, the leave-me-alone nature of scraping a living out of the very canyons whose beauty attracts travelers from around the world. I wished there were a bridge between these seemingly different worldviews that could move us across the chasm of "us versus them"—but it's a difficult bridge to find, even harder to build or to hold within one's own heart.

But in May 2003, when I checked into Boulder Mountain Lodge, something had changed. It felt different. I looked around. An elegant, lush garden with a statue of Buddha in the center greeted me. Day lilies waved in the breeze. Prayer flags hung outside Hell's Backbone Grill. And then I remembered hearing about the two women who had taken over the restaurant a few years earlier. Word was these women were outsiders like the rest of us. Only different. They came to Boulder not just to hike and commune with the desert, but to live and work. They hired the children of local ranchers, grew most of their own food, and created recipes that corresponded to what was available in each season. And no, they were not Mormons, like 90 percent of those who lived in Boulder, but somehow that didn't matter.

These two women, I found out later that night at dinner, are Blake Spalding and Jen Castle. They came to Boulder from Flagstaff, Arizona, with enormous skill developed during years of cooking for commercial river companies and in other remote camps around the American West. They brought with them baskets of instinct and secrets about the power of food and its potential for glory.

Blake sat down with us at our table. Our eyes met. We shared stories. She told of going to the town council meeting shortly after they arrived in Boulder and explaining how in order to make this restaurant a viable business, they would need a liquor license. This issue had come up before the town on a previous occasion with different restaurant owners and had been deeply divisive within the community.

The women conveyed their respect for Mormon beliefs and that they meant no harm. The community listened to the calm, thoughtful approach of this new enterprise that promised to feed an open spirit of cooperation in town. Finally, one of the LDS councilmen said, "Nobody ever talked to us like this before; they only yelled." He paused. "I am going to have to think hard about this."

Hell's Backbone Grill received its liquor license, and its doors have been open ever since, delighting travelers who come for rest and sanctuary at Boulder Mountain Lodge. The locals are developing a particular pride around the restaurant. It has become an oasis in the desert.

I stood outside after dinner, watching dusk glow on the cliffs before they turned dark and disappeared. Call it the encore light that glistens long after the sun sets. I took in deep breaths, aware of the fresh mint recently planted, and thought about how good this place felt, how peaceful, with much of the rawness and glares gone, and how change is possible when two people accept the power they have to make a difference in the world. Blake and Jen brought something with them when they came to Boulder, Utah— something that cannot be measured or named. Call it spirit or Knowledge with a capital "K" or just plain guts, but whatever their gifts, they allow us to see the magic that occurs when we choose to come to a place with an intention to create beauty.

What I love most about Hell's Backbone Grill is its ongoing story of restoration and reconciliation within a community known for its contention. It is not easy to enter a new town, especially a town like Boulder, Utah, that prides itself on insiders, locals, and natives. Genealogy is the primary ticket for access. And it is especially difficult to enter a Mormon community in the outback and ask for a liquor license, a request that first rolls down the aisle of the church like a cherry bomb, threatening to shatter the dominant culture's "Word of Wisdom" that forbids coffee, tea, and alcohol.

But this is exactly what Blake Spalding and Jen Castle did in the spring of 2000. They asked the citizens of Boulder, Utah, for a spiritual accommodation.

"We listened," said Blake. "We listened to the people who lived here and shared our belief in a vision of beautiful food in beautiful country. Many folks said we were crazy, that we wouldn't be able to find staff, that we wouldn't be able to keep our doors open in such remote country. But both Jen and I felt called to this landscape."

I thought about that bridge I had been wishing for and realized that a bridge might be too fragile and therefore temporary. What Blake and Jen have quietly done is fill in that gap, that dividing space between neighbors, with mindfulness. And they have filled it with the sacred nature of food.

The Buddha says breathing is a "quivering intake of life." At Hell's Backbone Grill, so is eating.

There are many forms of grace, especially in the desert. It is a landscape of prayers where one falls on hands and knees in gratitude for the splash of water that is not a mirage.

Hell's Backbone Grill is a place of such grace. It is water in the desert. The name is harsh like the country. But if you dare to enter in, dust off your shoulders, and let your eyes adjust to the peace inside, you will find within its unexpected embrace deep nourishment born out of struggle and love.

What lingers after a slow, thoughtful dinner is love. We are reminded through the creative hands of these believing women that daily renewal is possible through the loving gesture of a meal dreamed and shared.

Kayenta Ryan, full of grace.

ESCALANTE RIVER

Grace and Survival (Oh My Heck!)

All the world is a narrow bridge, and the most important thing is not to be afraid.

—TALMUDIC ADAGE

The word *grace* often seems to come with a silence attached to the end of it—a short pause like a beat in poetry or the moment of quiet after a song finishes. Perhaps this is because it's a meaningful word; the listener needs time to consider it. For many people, *grace* conjures up elegance, style, composure. To us, grace is an ethic as well, a central element of thoughtful, responsible daily interaction. And when we opened our restaurant, it was our goal. We wanted to run a viable business that embodied our shared principles and food philosophies, and to do it with passion, compassion, equanimity, generosity, loving kindness, and grace. We were unaware back then that given the unusual circumstances of our venture, this plan of action would also turn out to be our only chance of survival.

Hell's Backbone Grill takes its name from one of the most dramatic bridges in the world, a narrow, wooden engineering feat of a passage that straddles Box Death Hollow—one of Utah's more precarious and rugged corridors. Hell's Backbone Bridge first opened the town of Boulder to automobile travel when it was built in 1933. It's an apt name for us because the restaurant has been precisely that for the community: a bridge.

Our decision to open the kind of restaurant we envisioned in a remote, tiny, tightly knit community, most of whom are Mormon ranchers, was met with skepticism at first. In short, virtually everyone who loved us said we were crazy. They were too polite to say what they really thought, which was that we were stupid. But we did it anyway, and by taking the risk, discovered a community and home unlike anywhere else on earth.

Where we live—Boulder, Utah, population 180 (225 including the outskirts of town)—isn't even granted so much as a dot on most maps. A lot of people are certain we live in (ahem) Colorado. Boulder is located in south-central Utah, in the middle of the Grand Staircase-Escalante National Monument, approximately an hour and a half northeast of Bryce Canyon National Park and an hour south of Capitol Reef National Park. Boulder has no stoplight, no cell phone service, no ATM, no coffee shop, and no bar; no movie theater, video rental shop, medical facilities, or fast food. The nearest grocery store and bank are in Escalante, a forty-five minute drive over an awe-inspiring and slightly treacherous switchback road called the Hogsback, which has no guardrails and drops off almost vertically on both sides into vast, sweeping canyons.

What the community of Boulder does offer is a Mormon church, a post office, an elementary school, two gas stations, a handful of lodging options, three restaurants, one seasonal burger-and-ice-cream window, the Anasazi State Park Museum, Boulder Mountain Lodge (the eco-lodge on whose grounds the restaurant sits), more horses than citizens, stupefying natural beauty, and remarkable quantities of tolerance and kindheartedness.

Settled in 1889, an incorporated town since 1958, Boulder enjoys a wealth of delightful peculiarities. It didn't have electricity until 1947. It's been called the most remote town in the lower forty-eight states. With a population you could just about squeeze into a telephone booth, Boulder is ironically the largest town geographically in Utah after Salt Lake City. Also, as quiet as it appears from the outside, it's not unaccustomed to media attention or afraid to cause a ruckus—a ranching community located in one of America's last unspoiled lands, the town has been the subject of countless news stories highlighting public battles between ranchers and conservationists. However, Boulder's crowning claim is undoubtedly that it was the last town in America to stop receiving its mail by mule train, in 1942.

Boulder has seen significant changes since those days, particularly following President Clinton's 1996 designation of the surrounding 1.9 million acres as the Grand Staircase-Escalante National Monument—a move that took sixty years to approve and brought an influx of tourism, money, exposure, and controversy. Yet throughout it all, this old-fashioned, tenacious Mormon ranching community has somehow preserved its unique identity. Its ranchers and conservationists, while coexisting in reasonable peace, still don't quite see eye to eye. Today it remains one of the country's most inaccessible towns and continues to host more than its share of idiosyncrasies. We love that we're one of them.

We moved to Boulder from Flagstaff, Arizona, in the spring of 2000. Before that, Blake was working as a caterer and backcountry chef, and Jen was running the bakery at Macy's, a European-style coffeehouse. We had both cooked on the Colorado River in the Grand Canyon, but we didn't actually meet until a Christmas party, where we found ourselves devouring each other's dishes—Jen had brought posole and Blake a chicken liver pâté. It was an instant food-related affinity that swiftly developed into a strong friendship. Soon after meeting, we spent a month together in Washington State cooking for a Discovery Channel crew. We realized then that our food philosophies were identical, our values and humor compatible. After catering together several more times, the opportunity to own the grill was presented to Blake, who immediately asked Jen to be her business partner.

We instantly recognized it to be much more than a promising business opportunity—it was adventure, and more than anything, freedom. We were being given the chance to go far away from everyone we knew, to an isolated location where we'd be anonymous and could cook and serve whatever we pleased and put our theories into practice. We wanted to run a restaurant with heart, and to do so organically and with environmental awareness. We would follow Buddhist principles of right livelihood. We would offer only place-based, regionally relevant cuisine made from scratch. We would source locally for produce and employees and serve as an example of responsible growth in a town in need of economic stimulus. The circumstances were abnormal, yes, but we were river chefs and adept at making do. Improvisation was our specialty. Our unique skills, born of remote backcountry cooking experience, brought confidence, and we felt ready. How hard

could it possibly be? we thought. There would be running water, lights, and weekly food delivery—lavish compared to many of our previous work situations. We were certain we would be utterly happy and wildly successful.

So began our odyssey and cultural immersion. Concerned about offending the close-knit Mormon community in any way and determined to be respectful, at first we vowed to adjust our behavior. "We won't swear," we agreed as we drove to Boulder in the middle of the night with the dogs in the front of the old Ford truck, listening to Madonna and Prince. "We won't drink in front of them or dance—is dancing even legal in Utah?" We turned the music up louder and drove across the state line. This move represented a radical shift in lifestyle. But we would fit in. We'd prove our good manners and our willingness to adapt—the last thing we wanted was to be outsiders.

At the same time, it wasn't in us to be obsequious or ingratiating—we were who we were, and Mormons we were really not. We were women who used bad language in private, were raised in unorthodox families, and had treated ourselves to myriad world experiences. How could we strike a balance between who we were as people and what we wanted our neighbors to know of us? We finally decided to simply be ourselves and to enter the community with open minds and kind hearts. We would start by just being nice.

Jen Castle

Give me books, French wine, fruit, fine weather and a little music played out of doors by somebody I do not know.

—JOHN KEATS

Jennifer Castle never learned to cook for just one. Growing up in Albuquerque she was taught to prepare New Mexican cuisine by her mother and twelve aunts and uncles, who viewed mass-quantity cooking as standard procedure. As a child, a large part of Jen's free time was spent experimenting with food. "Other kids might go sneak a smoke in the woodshed," she says. "I practiced deep-frying sopapillas." Jen taught herself to cook by imitating the tastes she'd grown up around, always making enough for a crowd, and eventually adults began asking the secrets of her red chile beans, her chocolate chip cookies. Later, when she applied to work at Macy's European Coffee House, Bakery and Vegetarian Restaurant, a Flagstaff institution, the only food-related experience on her resume was a wedding for which she'd baked cookies for two hundred. At Macy's she learned about ordering, organizing, and time management. She taught herself to write recipes, manipulate ingredients, multitask like a maniac, and cook five major items simultaneously.

Halfway through Jen's stint at Macy's, she began a job in the Grand Canyon, cooking daily meals for thirty trail-crew workers, into the dead of winter. Subsequent river and backcountry trips honed her outdoor catering skills. Meanwhile, she grew friendships based on a shared work ethic. And as her world experience broadened, so did her food repertoire. She traveled to foreign countries and returned with journals full of culinary inspiration, eager to re-create the tastes she'd encountered abroad. Everywhere Jen turned in life, she was surrounded by ingredients, people, and possibilities, and perceived limitations such as lack of money or time constraints were challenges she met with pleasure. Over the years, she built up a reservoir of innovation and ability, a skill set that would eventually prove invaluable for cooking in yet another remote location—Boulder, Utah.

When Jen made the decision to move to Boulder she was at the crossroads phase in her life that so many almost-thirty-year-olds encounter. "I was ready for my next big thing, looking for a big city where I'd wear nice skirts and carry smart handbags and never, ever smell like sautéed onions again," she recalls. "But this business opportunity arose, and I realized that saying no would be more dangerous than saying yes. Fail and I'd still succeed, succeed and I'd be a success. Something like that. I knew that wherever it took me, I would be enriched. And then, there I was: owner of a restaurant in the middle of nowhere, smelling a lot like grilled steak."

For years Jen had cooked professionally as an easy, enjoyable way to access cool people, freedom, and travel opportunities; however, she wanted her work to have value in the world and wondered, was cooking really enough? She viewed her move to an extremely remote desert town as an incubation period; time to grow and discover what was next, away from everything she knew. It took three years in Boulder before she realized that she was born to cook, and that she was in exactly the right place.

Throughout her life, Jen has used food as a creative outlet and a way to express love. "I love thrilling people with food," she says, "and being thrilled by it. I take many steps creating dishes, with care and intention in every moment, every morsel. I'm particular about my ingredients and conscious of my audience—I cook with the eater in mind to give it some love juju. I'm at my happiest when I've made a pot of green chile stew that has my friends freaking out. And then they do the dishes."

Opening a restaurant and living in a community the size of Boulder provided Jen the rare opportunity to create food every day while embarking on a measured journey, albeit a mapless one, toward the development and realization of her personal ethic. "There's an enormous amount of freedom here," she says, "because the only thing people really notice, the only thing that impresses them, is how hard you work. You have to be nice and neighborly, but otherwise, there aren't many rules. My free time is wholly mine, and what people notice is my work—and it's incredibly affirming to be so deeply invested in what I do for a living; to create a product that's such an expression of myself. I've come to understand that doing what I do under these conditions and in this location is unquestionably worthwhile and meaningful. I love my life."

Blake Spalding

One day many years ago, Blake was in the backseat of a car heading to the airport with her Tibetan teacher, Chagdud Tulku Rinpoche, affectionately and respectfully known to his students as Rinpoche. She had been cooking for him in Colorado, where he was giving a Buddhist teaching. Suddenly, from the front seat of the car, he turned and fixed her with a powerful look. "It's good that you're a cook," he said in his strong accent. "This is really good work for you. There's no nonvirtue, only benefit. You make people happy." It became clear to Blake at that moment that it was time for her to apply herself to her longtime dream of opening a restaurant.

"The most significant thing that ever happened to me," Blake says, "was meeting Rinpoche. I feel tremendously grateful to him and can barely imagine what my life would be like if I hadn't met him. I give him a lot of credit for helping me achieve my goals. He passed away last year, but the time I spent with him and the things he taught me influenced every area of my life."

Because of her spiritual beliefs, Blake begins her morning meditation with the aspiration to be of benefit to others, and orients her day and her life to be able to do so. "Nothing makes me happier," she says. "I really love to cook. I've loved to cook since I was a small child, and the act of offering someone food is tremendously satisfying to me. When Jen and I first had the restaurant it was hard to get accustomed to the idea of charging people, because we were used to making food and giving it away. That's been the most complicated part of owning this restaurant—controlling our impulse to operate it like an ongoing dinner party."

Blake's mother, a talented cook, taught her how to cook when she was young and gave her enough freedom in the kitchen that by the age of eight she was preparing full meals for her family. She spent much of her life cooking and before moving to Boulder, worked for many years as a river chef, mostly on the Colorado River in the Grand Canyon. Every night for sixteen nights she set up a kitchen on a different beach and prepared dinner for twenty people, often in inclement weather. Each morning, she woke up early, cooked breakfast, took everything down, and packed it up in time to leave again before the sun hit camp.

"I became fast, efficient, and organized. And it takes a lot to rattle me now, because I've seen just about everything that could go wrong in a kitchen—fires, floods, wind, and all manner of chaos. Once, I had a tug-of-war with a ringtail cat who was trying to steal a two-pound bag of roast beef."

Blake equates running the grill, in a certain respect, to a four-year river trip. "River trips," she points out, "are incredibly intense. You truly get to know the people you work with, as you put in incredibly long hours together with no respite." She finds that people who work on the river have a tremendous opportunity for self-examination and self-awareness because, stripped of the things that usually define them, such as possessions and homes, they're just people who get up, work all day, try to have fun and be good, help others, go to sleep, get up, and do it again. What comes through about them is their work ethic, their value systems, and the way they react under pressure. "The relationships I forged with people on the river are to this day some of my strongest," Blake says. "I feel the same about my relationships with people at the restaurant, because what really come to bear are the same qualities of how hard you work, how kind you are, how much you laugh."

Blake took a sabbatical from the river for a time to work for the international environmental organization Greenpeace. An anti-pesticide campaign she worked on became the genesis of her passion for all things organic and biochemically and genetically unaltered.

At the same time she began doing volunteer work for an international peace-building organization called Project RAFT (Russians and Americans For Teamwork) that worked through the bonding medium of whitewater rafting. Here she was trained by some of the foremost minds in facilitation and conflict resolution. "When I was working with Project RAFT, I became fascinated with the dynamic that evolves out of mixing cultures and the ensuing process of discovering commonality. I had no idea at the time how valuable this training would prove."

Blake had been working as a river guide for about six years when, floating downstream on a raft in the Grand Canyon, she received a fax delivered to her by another raft, offering her a job cooking on a deserted island in the Exuma Keys in the Bahamas

We ask our employees not to harm any living creatures at the restaurant. A "bug catcher" with a detachable lid is a kinder approach to removing the occasional flying visitor. It allows the user to gently vacuum the insect then release it outdoors.

for MTV's *The Real World* television show. It was then that her niche was born—extreme catering.

"My specialty became doing fresh food in isolated places," Blake says. "I've had supplies brought to me by dugout canoe, helicopter, and small plane, and I've waited for food to arrive on the back of a mule." Blake was called when it was impossible to get a normal caterer and when the job presented seemingly insurmountable obstacles—no refrigeration, no running water, no clean sources of water, or no water at all, as in the Bahamas (where there was only saltwater). It was difficult work that began with designing a menu to meet many different needs—people who had unusual diets, vegetarians, and vegans, as well as teens who wanted only basic food. Then she had to source the food. "I had one job in Suriname that was especially tricky," she says, "because I had to go to the main city and shop for three days in a language I didn't speak, to cook food in the middle of the Amazon rain forest for three weeks." And of course she had to pack the food, deliver it to the remote location, keep it safe from animals and heat with no refrigeration, and prepare it under adverse circumstances. "One night I had forty-five minutes of sleep," she says, "because I was working the other twenty-three hours and fifteen minutes."

In addition to extreme catering and backcountry cooking, Blake owned and operated a catering business in Flagstaff and often cooked for Tibetan lamas. "One of the things I've learned cooking for the lamas," she says, "is that what your mind's doing while you're cooking is important. I'm of the opinion that food has memory. Cooking in an unhappy or angry state of mind affects the way the body experiences the food. I think if you're in a terrible mood making soup, there's a good chance the soup will cause heartburn or a stomachache. I've learned to meditate while cooking to infuse the food with a quality of loving kindness and generosity. It's the way you're trained in a Buddhist retreat center—to establish a loving intention in your mind when cooking."

... And Restaurant Makes Three

Be favorable to bold beginnings.

—VIRGIL

Helles* B. Bone was born in the year 2000 when, too broke to buy CDs for our new restaurant, we created her as an imaginary identity in order to get twelve free CDs from a music club. To this day we still receive credit card offers for her.

It was certainly appropriate in the beginning to give the grill a nickname—she was our squawking infant, our newborn adopted orphan who kept us up all night. We didn't know how to make her happy, couldn't figure out what she needed. We displayed all the telltale signs of new parents: bags and circles under our eyes, unmatched clothing, quick tempers, a surfeit of pride, and constant confusion and panic. "Helles," we'd say to each other, "is showing some early signs of behavioral problems." "When is she going to be potty trained?" "I think Helles has ADHD." "What is wrong with her?"

"The first thing you should understand," Blake likes to tell new employees she's training, "is that Helles is our child. At times a little difficult, slightly neurotic, overdramatic, and spoiled, but we're extremely attached to her and her well-being. The only way it'll work for you to have a job here is if you strive to love her deeply as well. Any indication of neglect or lack of enthusiasm will make it really hard for us to get along."

If Helles were a human, she'd be a stubborn five-year-old, part-Buddhist, part-Mormon, and part hellion, who craved silence but made an outlandish amount of noise herself; who loved to meditate but needed to dance. She'd grow up to be one of the hardest workers ever. She would possess impeccable taste, incredible class, a silly and delightfully raunchy sense of humor, a deep-rooted appreciation for bluegrass music and top-forty boy bands, a desire to feed the world healthy, delicious, interesting food, and during the busy seasons, a serious potential for kava kava dependency.

Oh, our little girl, she's growing up so fast.

* Rhymes with "fellas."

Spring

Spring

*A little madness in the Spring is wholesome
even for the King.*

—EMILY DICKINSON

Our season officially begins in March, a time of year considered spring in other regions of America. Not in Boulder. At over 6,700 feet elevation, it's more like the end of winter here—still chilly, with some wildly gorgeous days followed by the occasional death-to-seedlings frost. In March things are just beginning to pulsate, and we're bracing ourselves for the eight months ahead. We have severe sleep deprivation to look forward to, and its natural corollaries of caffeine abuse and ugly sugar crashes. There's the unending, desperate search for staff; countless meals to cook and serve; and the sobering reality of our new schedule: wake up at six, return home at midnight, wake up at six. Wash, rinse, and repeat.

Over the next nine months, we'll make each other laugh so hard we choke, get so angry we cry. We'll complain and congratulate and sing and survive, and then, at the end of it all, be rewarded with another glorious, silent winter—for it would be wrong and an absolute corruption of the truth to deny that when we open in March we aren't already looking forward—just a teeny bit—to closing in November. It's not that we don't love our little restaurant Helles with every bit of our hearts, because we absolutely do. We've put so much into her. It's just that when you run a restaurant like ours, sleep gets to be something you only barely remember doing. It becomes little more than a beautiful fabled concept you talk about in the kitchen while waiting for the French press to brew, eating a chocolate chile cream pot for breakfast.

At the beginning of the season we're still a bit fuzzy around the edges, but there's also a palpable energy rekindling the place. We spend a lot of time flipping through cookbooks and food magazines, reading recipes for inspiration and studying the inside of the freezer, contemplating what can be made out of two hundred pounds of frozen lamb, a box of squash, and nine artichokes. It's our most challenging time to create a menu. Food is hard to come by this early in the season, so we rely heavily on Mountain People's Co-op deliveries and what garden produce we've frozen in anticipation of opening. A typical early spring menu might include juniper lamb posole as an entrée, and under the small-plates selections, a filo-wrapped winter squash, spinach, and Utah goat-cheese pastry. For dessert, old-fashioned

Spring

Spring

A little madness in the Spring is wholesome even for the King.

—EMILY DICKINSON

Our season officially begins in March, a time of year considered spring in other regions of America. Not in Boulder. At over 6,700 feet elevation, it's more like the end of winter here—still chilly, with some wildly gorgeous days followed by the occasional death-to-seedlings frost. In March things are just beginning to pulsate, and we're bracing ourselves for the eight months ahead. We have severe sleep deprivation to look forward to, and its natural corollaries of caffeine abuse and ugly sugar crashes. There's the unending, desperate search for staff; countless meals to cook and serve; and the sobering reality of our new schedule: wake up at six, return home at midnight, wake up at six. Wash, rinse, and repeat.

Over the next nine months, we'll make each other laugh so hard we choke, get so angry we cry. We'll complain and congratulate and sing and survive, and then, at the end of it all, be rewarded with another glorious, silent winter—for it would be wrong and an absolute corruption of the truth to deny that when we open in March we aren't already looking forward—just a teeny bit—to closing in November. It's not that we don't love our little restaurant Helles with every bit of our hearts, because we absolutely do. We've put so much into her. It's just that when you run a restaurant like ours, sleep gets to be something you only barely remember doing. It becomes little more than a beautiful fabled concept you talk about in the kitchen while waiting for the French press to brew, eating a chocolate chile cream pot for breakfast.

At the beginning of the season we're still a bit fuzzy around the edges, but there's also a palpable energy rekindling the place. We spend a lot of time flipping through cookbooks and food magazines, reading recipes for inspiration and studying the inside of the freezer, contemplating what can be made out of two hundred pounds of frozen lamb, a box of squash, and nine artichokes. It's our most challenging time to create a menu. Food is hard to come by this early in the season, so we rely heavily on Mountain People's Co-op deliveries and what garden produce we've frozen in anticipation of opening. A typical early spring menu might include juniper lamb posole as an entrée, and under the small-plates selections, a filo-wrapped winter squash, spinach, and Utah goat-cheese pastry. For dessert, old-fashioned strawberry rhubarb shortcake with fresh whipped cream.

In terms of gardening, spring is a pivotal, action-packed season that keeps us quite busy. Our gardeners start by removing winter's debris—dead flower stalks and leaves mostly—and do some early planting; we start tomatoes, lettuce, tomatillos, and peppers (jalapeño, Anaheim, and poblano) from seed in flats and put the hardier vegetables (spinach, broccoli, beets, carrots, and peas) into the ground. Other seeds go in later, when frost is no longer a threat: melons, corn, cucumber, Swiss chard, pumpkins, and cauliflower, to name a few.

The restaurant remains relatively quiet for the first few weeks, so we spend time cleaning it up while we still can, before the noise begins. The dining room at the grill is tasteful but simple—with a backdrop like Boulder, elaborate decorations would be excessive. The building is hogan-style, with bare, unfinished pine beams and tall windows looking out onto sandstone buttes. Our tables are made of wood with polished, acid-treated galvanized metal tops, and each one holds flowers and a candle. On the walls we display work by two exceptionally talented friends: Scotty Mitchell, a local woman who works mostly with pastels, and Sam Jones, a native Utahan watercolorist who now lives in Flagstaff. One of our servers—usually our golden boy, BJ—will climb a twelve-foot ladder to dust the wooden ceiling beams, while someone else washes the windows. Meanwhile, we'll unveil the CD mixes we've each burned over the winter in an attempt to entertain the staff members as they clean.

By April, we're well into our groove, and the restaurant is thrumming. Warm weather brings our first major rush of tourists, and outside the restaurant, an astounding act of nature occurs. Wildflowers suddenly bloom in every color and size; yellow-headed blackbirds, coots, herons, Canada geese, and migrating waterfowl land in the bird sanctuary outside our kitchen door, and hummingbirds hang in the air by the feeders on the deck. We harvest kale, salad greens, and fresh herbs from the garden. The sky each day is a vibrant, crystalline blue, and at dusk, 360-degree pink and orange sunsets wrap softly around the edges of town. At night, more stars than you've ever imagined.

By this time, the season has taken hold of us—we're tightly focused, basically inaccessible to our friends and family, and speaking a language that sounds strange and slightly disturbing to anyone outside the restaurant business. The dining room is packed at night, the kitchen is pure madness, and we are growing tired beyond human comprehension. Jen goes to the dentist for a crown replacement and is given novocaine and a second anesthetic (this one containing adrenaline), and while they have her mouth cranked wide open and are drilling away at her tooth, she falls into a sound sleep. That's how tired we are.

We're being pulled along firmly by Helles's strong little hands. We're a third of the way there.

Boulder Mountain Lodge:
The Home of Hell's Backbone Grill

Spend ten minutes at Boulder Mountain Lodge, and it's easy to understand why it was named one of the top ten adventure lodges in the world by *Outside Traveler* magazine, why it was voted "Best Civilized Escape" by *Salt Lake* magazine: there's the fifteen-acre bird sanctuary fluttering with great blue herons, yellow-headed blackbirds, coots, and mallards; the rustic, elegant western architecture of red stucco, rose-colored sandstone blocks, giant spruce timbers, and dramatically pitched rusted metal roofs; the gorgeous Craftsman-style wooden furniture in the twenty guest rooms. But what really makes the lodge remarkable is what happens when one spends more than ten minutes there. It's the unexpected transformation invoked in countless guests who come to sightsee and stay to exhale.

Many arrive with big plans—they want to go horseback riding and fly-fishing, they say. They'd like to hit Bryce Canyon and Capitol Reef, the Burr Trail and Hole in the Rock. They've got to hike Calf Creek Falls, and the guidebook says something about Anasazi rock art. What should they do first, they ask? Do they have time to see it all? And by the way, how far is it to town? They haven't yet realized they're standing in the heart of it.

By the second day there's a subtle change—shoulders have loosened. They return from day trips tan and smiling, bones tired but minds awake. They want to sit on their balconies and look out on the sandstone mesas, read up on the history of this ancient place, buy more film and better hiking shoes, maybe even talk to someone about real estate. And if the lodge isn't full, they'd like to book another night, pretty please. The fact is there's nothing even vaguely typical about these accommodations or this town. Boulder makes a permanent impression; it folds itself tightly into visitors' memories, and year after year they come back.

The lodge, built in 1994, is owned by Dave Mock, a venture capitalist who has cofounded and started more than twenty companies. Dave grew up in southern California and now lives most of the year in Salt Lake City. He discovered Boulder in 1960 on an excursion with his parents. "We came over Hell's Backbone and Boulder Mountain," he recalls, "and I thought it was the grandest place I'd ever been in my life."

The decisions Dave makes regarding the lodge are oriented, he says, to building a place where families can experience the area while becoming educated about efforts to preserve and conserve the pristine resources. "I'm a strong wilderness advocate," he says. "I believe in sustainable economics. I believe that changes in the economic models in rural America impact peoples' attitudes about how to protect their natural treasures. The key is sustainability, and providing sustainability through ecotourism is a great way to start the process. Being involved with a sustainable model, like an eco-lodge, can influence a way of thinking and help people to be more conservation-minded."

Dave's goal is to provide a point-of-destination resort that allows people to connect with the area. "I want my guests to notice that they're in one of the most beautiful places on earth, and that the quality of this place depends on them. They need to interact with a place to love it—they have to touch it and really be in it. They can't do it from afar. The lodge provides a home base from which they can go out and develop that kind of relationship with the land."

Although the restaurant and lodge are separate businesses, they have a strong symbiotic relationship. Without Dave Mock, Helles would be little more than a twinkle in our eyes. He's our eternal advocate, always open to change and suggestions. He supports positive-growth avenues in Boulder, has a kind heart, and is the perfect example of someone who uses his power for good, not evil.

"There's a synergy between the lodge and the grill," Dave says. "The lodge and the restaurant have benefited each other, because we provide a comfortable place to stay—a getaway with all the amenities—and Jen and Blake provide high-quality food from organic sources and a friendly, hands-on, personal atmosphere. It all works together, and the main reason is that Blake, Jen, and I share conservationist views. We're kindred spirits, all interested in the preservation of the land. We see it as something sacred."

Desert Sage Flatbread

With fresh garden sage and a sprinkle of salt, no creature can resist this bread. Preheat oven to 350 degrees.

> 3 cups warm water
> 1 tablespoon yeast
> 1 tablespoon sugar
> 6 cups flour
> 1¼ cups cornmeal
> ½ cup bran
> ¼ cup olive oil plus more for drizzling
> 1 tablespoon salt plus coarse salt for sprinkling
> 2 tablespoons chopped fresh sage

1. In a large mixing bowl combine the water, yeast, and sugar and let bubble for 10 minutes.

2. Add flour, cornmeal, bran, oil, salt, and sage to yeast mixture. Mix slowly, as it can get messy. Machine-knead for 5 minutes, or knead by hand until dough is smooth and easy to handle.

3. Place dough in large, oiled bowl. Turn dough ball to coat with oil and cover with plastic wrap. Let rise 30 minutes.

4. Re-knead for a minute, adding additional flour if necessary to make the dough easier to handle. Pull dough out onto floured table and form into 6-ounce balls (tennis-ball-sized) for sandwiches, or 3-ounce balls (golf-ball-sized) for dinner rolls. Place balls on lined baking sheet and flatten a bit. Let rise 10 minutes, then flatten again, spreading dough with fingertips and poking small holes into surface. Bread should be flat and round, like a hamburger bun. Drizzle more olive oil over tops of formed flatbread and sprinkle them with coarse salt. For an extra zing add chile flakes or grated Parmesan. The poked holes will collect the sprinkled goodies, creating lovely pockets of flavor.

5. Bake flatbread 25 to 35 minutes until golden and fragrant.

Apricot-Almond Breakfast Bread Pudding

This spicy, chunky, fruity concoction with a brickle-sugar top is best enjoyed warm with freshly whipped cream. (Spike it with a smitch of bourbon for a swoony grown-up dessert!)

Baked gently in a water bath, the pudding's edges stay as moist as its insides. Bake your own loaf of bread a day ahead or use leftover odd pieces from the freezer.

> 1 cup dried sour cherries, roughly chopped
> ½ cup dried apricots or ½ cup dried cranberries, chopped
> ½ cup brandy
> ¼ cup hot water
> 1 loaf white bread (about 10 cups of torn pieces)
> 2 cups half & half
> 2 cups heavy cream
> 6 eggs
> 1 tablespoon vanilla extract
> 1 cup white sugar
> ¾ cup brown sugar
> 2 tablespoons cinnamon
> 1 teaspoon nutmeg
> 1 teaspoon salt
> 1½ cups sliced almonds
> additional 1 cup white sugar

1. Soak the cherries and apricots in ½ cup boiling water and ½ cup brandy for 1 hour.

2. Slice bread, then cut or tear slices into large rough chunks and place in large mixing bowl.

3. In medium bowl, combine half & half, cream, eggs, vanilla, sugars, and spices. Pour over bread. Add soaked fruit with its liquid, and nuts. Combine well.

4. Pour into a buttered, high-sided 9" square baking dish or a 9 x 12" dish. Let sit half an hour to soak up the custard.

5. Cover top of pudding with the additional ¾ cup sugar and cover dish with a buttered piece of foil. Place covered pan in a second baking dish, one size larger. Fill larger dish with water. Bake 60 minutes at 350 degrees in this water bath, adding more water as needed. Remove foil and bake 20 to 30 minutes longer, till top is shiny and hard.

Oatmeal Molasses Bread

This is Blake's great-great-grandmother Ella Jane Blodgett's recipe. Blake has been making this bread since she was ten years old. The smell of it baking might just bring tears of joy to your eyes.

¾ cup organic rolled oats
¼ cup organic steel-cut oats
2 cups boiling water
2 tablespoons melted butter
½ cup plus 2 tablespoons molasses
2 teaspoons salt
I tablespoon dry yeast
½ cup lukewarm water
5½ cups unbleached organic bread flour

1. Pour the water over the oats in a large bread bowl and let stand for an hour. Add in melted butter, salt, and molasses.

2. In a separate bowl, add 1 tablespoon yeast to ½ cup lukewarm water with 2 tablespoons molasses mixed in. Let this mixture rest and bloom (about 10 minutes), then add to the oats mixture.

3. Mix in 5½ cups unbleached organic bread flour. Watch dough and add a little flour as necessary to get a perfect tacky-but-not-sticky texture.

4. Knead dough well for 10 minutes or so. If your dough is on the dry side, knead it on an oiled board. If it gets too sticky, knead in a little flour.

5. Butter bowl and top of dough ball and cover it up with a wet towel. Let it rise in a warm place for two hours or until doubled in size.

6. Punch it down, shape it into two loaves, and place loaves into buttered pans. Let them rest for at least a half hour or until doubled in size.

7. Preheat oven to 425 degrees. Put loaves into hot oven for 10 minutes then reduce heat to 350 degrees and cook for another 35 minutes or so. If they sound hollow when tapped, they're done.

8. Pop them out of their pans and cool on a rack or a towel.

Strawberry Freezer Jam

This recipe was shared with us by our local postmistress and very dear friend, Judi Davis. We have found that the same technique works just as well for various types of fruit, including plums, apricots, cherries, and peaches. We freeze all the jams, butters, compotes, and chutneys we make for later use at the restaurant.

14 cups crushed strawberries (mash with potato masher or gently pulse in a food processor)
2½ cups turbinado sugar
juice of 2 lemons
2 teaspoons sea salt
4 tablespoons dry pectin

Combine everything in a heavy-bottomed, medium-sized pot. Bring pot slowly to boil (20 minutes), stirring occasionally. Cool jam, portion it out into freezer-safe containers, cover tightly, and freeze.

In the Words of Chagdud Tulku Rinpoche

Chagdud Tulku Rinpoche

His Eminence Chagdud Tulku Rinpoche, Blake's primary teacher of Buddhism, was a highly revered Tibetan meditation master born in 1930 in eastern Tibet. In 1959 Rinpoche, as he was respectfully and affectionately known by his students, fled Tibet during the consolidation of power by the communist Chinese. For the next twenty years, he helped develop Tibetan refugee communities in India and Nepal. In 1979 Rinpoche came to the United States and established Chagdud Gonpa Foundation, named after his monastery in eastern Tibet. Over the years, he created numerous centers throughout the world for the study and practice of Vajrayana Buddhism. In 1996 Rinpoche moved to Brazil, where the vast range of his activity continued to grow. He taught tirelessly through the very evening of his passing in November 2002.

In *Change of Heart,* Padma Publishing, 2003, compiled and edited by Lama Shenpen Drolma, Rinpoche talks about how to bring the practice of loving kindness into our daily lives.

"Ideally, we would use our short time in the human realm to bring joy and happiness to each other's lives. This is love—the aspiration that others find happiness. The mere assertion that we should love each other has little value; we need to exemplify loving kindness. Recognizing that others need and want happiness just as we do, we concentrate increasingly on their wishes rather than our own. Expressing our love for those we hold close, as well as for those less familiar to us, can make a difference in our family and community and set an example for the next generation.

"We can practice selflessness very directly by bringing an altruistic motivation to all our relationships. Entering into a relationship in the hope that the other person will make us happy will produce a very different result than approaching it with the sincere desire to work for the other's well-being. Depending on someone else for contentment makes it hard for a relationship to endure. Instead of expecting others to meet our needs, we should ask ourselves how we can best fulfill theirs. That simple shift in focus amounts to great [spiritual] practice.

"If we are genuinely altruistic toward one another and constantly strive to meet each other's needs, the bonds between us cannot be broken. When we work for the happiness of others, they will come to value and respect us. Their appreciation will naturally translate into kindness and helpfulness toward others, as well as toward us. Even if we tried to push people away, they wouldn't leave because they would be so drawn to our loving kindness.

"Because we are familiar with the needs of those we know well, we can find many opportunities to help and inspire them with our thoughts, words, and actions. Think of how much pleasure we derive from a gentle, meaningful conversation or are warmed by a friend's generosity in giving us a cup of tea. We too can offer sources of simple joy to our friends. Whether or not others reciprocate isn't the point. Usually, we are far too immersed in the idea that if I scratch your back, you have to scratch mine. A relationship will never work if there is a balance sheet nailed to the door. By serving those in our lives with pure motivation, we ultimately serve all beings through the virtue we create and dedicate to their welfare.

"Acting out of self-interest, attachment, and aversion is like cooking with a filthy pot. No matter how appealing the ingredients, or how long and carefully we cook them, the pot will only spoil the food. Self-clinging establishes a boundary between ourselves—including all we take to be ours—and everything else. We tend to isolate what we believe, need, and want for ourselves from the beliefs, needs, and desires of others. Such attachment leads to fixation on our own ideas, family, community, or country. We exaggerate the value of whatever we call 'mine,' imagining ourselves and 'ours' to be uniquely important. This perspective separates, binds, and restricts us, making openness impossible.

"Although we may aspire to help [others], we often find ourselves hampered by negativity and mental habits that perpetuate suffering and conflict rather than create happiness and harmony. Our intention to aid someone we sympathize with might be compromised by aversion toward someone who has injured her or by our desire to gain or achieve something through our actions. If in our efforts to help we become judgmental and self-righteous, if we angrily try to control or retaliate against someone, then our intention is tainted by pride and aversion. If our motivation for helping others is marred by desire, anger, or self-interest, we are like a doctor who administers sweet-tasting medicine laced with poison. It might seem delicious in the short run, but will ultimately only cause harm.

"The mind is like a fertile field. If we contaminate it with the poisons of ignorance, desire, anger, jealousy, and pride, we will inevitably produce poisonous crops. Acting carelessly or harmfully toward others, or working for our own benefit at the expense of others, will only create limitation and suffering. Medicinal seeds—wholesome, virtuous acts of kindness, love, and compassion—will produce the fruits of peace and benefit. Actions that are both positive and negative will produce a mixture

of happiness and sadness. Our thoughts give rise to words and actions, and these have consequences. We cannot plant poisonous seeds and expect edible or medicinal fruit. When we begin to see the negative results of our self-centeredness, we understand why we must carefully choose which seeds to plant.

"Good heart is the medicine that heals all conflict, the great antidote to selfishness and the problems that stem from it. It naturally gives rise to understanding and compassion; it makes us more open to listening, more able to see why we are having interpersonal problems and how to resolve them. As we give rise to good heart, we watch our own and others' happiness grow.

"We begin [to bring forth good heart] by cultivating pure motivation. Contemplating the experiences of those caught in cycles of suffering, we give rise to compassion and the aspiration to do whatever we can to help. But we need more than the wish to benefit. We may want to save a drowning person, but if we can't swim or don't have a boat or rope, we won't be of much use. We must learn to swim before we can save others. With the love and compassion now in our hearts, we might be able to help ten, twenty, a thousand, or maybe a hundred thousand people. But even that is not sufficient, for countless beings suffer in every moment. Despite our good intentions, our ability to help others is limited. Any positive impact we have will be temporary, because our spiritual capacity is so meager. We need to dedicate ourselves to expanding that capacity, to fully realizing our inherent positive qualities.

"Our true nature is a state of perfection imbued with wisdom, compassion, and the potential to create limitless benefit. For most of us, this nature is obscured, like a crystal encased in stone. We aren't omniscient and haven't completely developed our compassion and ability to help. However, through spiritual practice we can fully actualize these qualities. Increasing our love and compassion can be a goal for all of us, regardless of our spiritual tradition. Compassion and wisdom give rise to the power of ceaseless benefit. By applying spiritual methods to change our own mind, we develop an ever-greater ability to serve others. . . .

"Good heart is the essence of the [commitment in the Mahayana] Buddhist tradition—to free all beings from suffering, bring about their unending happiness, and undertake spiritual methods that will enable us to do so. In essence, [this] means that self-clinging and self-interest give way to unceasing concern for others. The ideal motivation, then, for [anything we do], is to fully reveal our true nature so that we may be of limitless benefit. Such motivation is selfless, pure, and exalted. The more we bring it to everything we do, the greater the scope and power of our actions. Tibetans have a saying: 'The dancer must follow the beat of the drum.' Upholding pure motivation in our lives lends beauty, power, and inspiration to the dance, and ensures true and lasting benefit."

Blue-Ribbon Biscuits

Bread is the warmest, kindest of words. Write it always with a capital letter, like your own name.

—RUSSIAN CAFÉ SIGN

Our black-powder cowboy biscuit, served as a complimentary accompaniment to dinner, holds a special place in our hearts. First, it won Jen a blue ribbon at the Coconino County Fair. It's also an absolute gold mine of culinary potential. In terms of minimizing waste and finding additional uses for that which we already have on hand, the biscuit is the uncontested kitchen champion—it continues feeding us long after it has served its original purpose of "Hey, look Hon, free bread!" Named for the combination of baking powder and black pepper in the recipe, our black-powder biscuit is served with whipped butter with freshly snipped sage. It's also delicious drizzled with some local honey, which we get from the Davis family, or dipped into a warm chocolate chile cream pot. It comes out of the kitchen hot and is served before every meal. Then the leftover biscuit goes into our meat loaf, is used as the base for the trout rub, becomes bread pudding, and thickens the creamed Swiss chard. And yeah, it's even good as a leftover biscuit.

The biscuit is one of those delicate culinary wonders that perhaps only a baker who has had his or her soul shattered by failed batches can truly appreciate. It can be made so beautifully by gentle, mindful hands, and there's something unquestionably sublime about a biscuit's fluff, its crumb, the trace of cornmeal on its skin. It can also, in an instant, turn on you and become the bane of your existence. The daily fresh biscuit routine tends to get tiresome, and the process of making multiple batches of biscuits will often consume hours and leave your kitchen looking like a fourth-grade home economics class. There's also the unfortunate reality that even a talented baker with fantastic style and meticulous technique can easily blow a batch by letting the dough warm up, using outdated baking powder, overmixing, or baking in a too-tepid oven. And a bad batch of biscuits is a sad, sad thing.

Our biscuit appears in a great many recipes—it's a lifesaver for us, the most versatile and accommodating of all our foodstuffs. You'll find it listed as an ingredient again and again and may feel dismayed because we have, perhaps, just now scared you away from making them (though you really should, they're

divine). When you come across a recipe that calls for biscuits, we absolutely encourage you to make a batch to eat with your dinner or for breakfast and to use in recipes for the rest of the week; however, you'll also do fine to substitute a nice store-bought French loaf or our milk bread.

Blue-Ribbon Black-Powder Buttermilk Biscuits

A very hot oven and very cold dough collaborate and conspire to bring you the fluffiest biscuit. A food processor fitted with a steel blade will mix the butter into the dry ingredients while keeping it cold and firm. Double this batch in order to secure leftovers you'll play with in other recipes.

3 tablespoons cornmeal
2½ cups white flour
1½ teaspoons salt
½ teaspoon baking soda
1 teaspoon baking powder
½ teaspoon coarse black pepper
1 teaspoon white sugar
¼ pound (1 stick) butter, chilled and cut into ½" chunks
1 cup buttermilk (substitute 1 cup milk with 2 teaspoons lemon juice)

1. Adjust oven rack to middle position and heat to 450 degrees. Grease 9 x 11" cookie sheet or line with parchment. Sprinkle 2 tablespoons cornmeal over surface.

2. Place flour, salt, baking soda, baking powder, pepper, and sugar in a large bowl or in the work bowl of a food processor fitted with a steel blade. Whisk together or pulse 5 to 7 times.

3. If making by hand, cut butter in with a pastry blender or 2 knives until the mixture resembles uneven, coarse crumbs. If using a food processor, distribute butter chunks over the dry ingredients. Pulse 10 to 12 times, then transfer to a large bowl.

4. Pour buttermilk over top of dough, folding ingredients at edges of bowl into middle using a rubber spatula or handy plastic dough scraper. Rotate bowl one-quarter turn with each fold until dough is moistened and sticky, leaving few dry patches.

5. Turn dough ball out onto lightly floured counter. Dust your hands with flour and gently ease dough into a square shape. With bench scraper or sharp kitchen knife, cut dough in half and stack one-half on top of the other. Repeat three times, flattening, cutting, and stacking, adding small amounts of flour if necessary to keep it from sticking.

6. Transfer stack to prepared cookie sheet. Sprinkle dough with remaining 1 tablespoon cornmeal. Using floured rolling pin, roll to 1" thick. Cut biscuits with knife or bench scraper into 2 x 2" squares. Bake until golden brown, about 15 minutes.

Variations on the theme...

CHEESY BACON BISCUITS
Follow the recipe for biscuits. After completing step 2, stir in ½ cup cheddar cheese cut into ¼" pieces and 3 strips fried bacon cut into ¼" pieces. Increase baking time to 18 minutes.

CINNAMON BREAKFAST BISCUITS
Mix ⅓ cup white sugar with 1 teaspoon cinnamon in small bowl. Follow the recipe for biscuits, sprinkling cinnamon mixture between each of the cut and stacked layers in step 5 as well as over the top. Omit final tablespoon of cornmeal.

Grill Meets Boy

Now I see the secret of the making of the best persons.
It is to grow in the open air and to eat and sleep with the earth.

—WALT WHITMAN

BJ Orozco arrived in Boulder in March of our second season and dropped his resume with the lodge secretary at the front desk. It was the middle of the afternoon, between shifts, so the restaurant was empty and the shutters closed. He came back to meet us the next afternoon, Thursday, around five o'clock. "As I walked to the grill in my best ranch clothes," he remembers, "I heard pop music pumping from the kitchen through the locked door, so I strolled around behind through the back gate and into the back door. There I met Lily (Jen's dog) for the first time in all her 'furrosity' and met Jen prancing through the kitchen with a fresh pan of biscuits." Despite the fact that BJ had no previous restaurant experience whatsoever, we hired him on the spot, and he started working the next day. It was an unprecedented decision and probably the finest one we made that year.

Perpetually good humored, kind, gentle, unflappable, absolutely gorgeous, and totally unpretentious—and quite possibly the love of Helles's life—BJ, twenty-eight years old from Tucson, Arizona, moved to Boulder with no other agenda than to exist for as long as possible in this land of jaw-dropping beauty. He was hired first to work as a llama trek guide, and he does that too, but in the beginning he mostly worked for us. We needed him; it was an insanely busy period compounded by the fact that we were pathetically understaffed. BJ slipped seamlessly into the frenetic rhythm of the kitchen and the grueling schedule, proving his mettle by uncomplainingly working each and every shift with us. We taught him to wait tables, but it didn't take much. Before we even got our hands on him, he was a server in the purest definition of the word: instinctually willing and helpful, interested in improving people's lives, and well equipped to do so.

After three weeks of marathon breakfasts, lunches, and dinners, Blake looked at him one afternoon and said, "BJ, we love you." "Well, it sure took you long enough," he answered without blinking. "I've loved you guys since the day I walked in here."

His first year in Boulder, BJ lived in his old reef-blue Volkswagen bus. With the help of his uncle, he'd installed solar panels on the top to run a refrigerator. He still drives the bus around Boulder but now lives in the communal restaurant trailer, where he's building a shade den with water features off the side of his bedroom. He spends a lot of time trekking through the canyons and learning primitive skills—he carves his own bows and makes arrowheads. He loves Marty Robbins and strong black tea with butter and salt, and he's teaching himself to play the mandolin. He knows where the best prehistoric rock art in the area is hidden and can tell you more than you ever wanted to know about the secret lives of llamas. He's been with us for four seasons now, and for that, our debt to the universe is inestimable.

"This is my first and last restaurant job," BJ says without hesitation. "There could be no other restaurant job better than this one. There's always something to learn from Blake and Jen—they have so much to give . . . to teach. My life has changed quite a bit since I moved here. Jen and Blake have shown me some amazing things about life, from business to relationships, ceaseless hard work to hearty good times. It was the surroundings that brought me here, but it's the girls that made me stay."

BJ continues to cheerfully work ridiculous hours at the grill. He still listens with inconceivable patience, never acting bothered if we talk too much, laugh too loudly, hiccup in the middle of a good cry. And he loves our pets—all seven of them. He feeds the cats, takes the dogs hiking and camping, bathes them, gives them haircuts, and watches them when we go on vacation. He's seen us both break down, and he's celebrated our triumphs with us. He's family.

Spiced Artichokes

Have fun with this recipe by experimenting with different spice combinations and potencies. We serve our artichokes as a springtime appetizer with the backbone sauce for dipping.

6 small artichokes
1 teaspoon whole cloves
10 juniper berries
4 bay leaves
4 stars of anise
1 teaspoon peppercorns
½ teaspoon red chile flakes (add more if you like the heat)
4 whole cloves garlic
2 teaspoons sea salt

1. Prepare artichokes: choose only firm, young, small, unspotted ones—these have the best flavor. Trim off stems, and use kitchen shears or scissors to cut spiky points off outside leaves. Rinse under cold water. Running half a lemon over outside of artichokes will prevent leaves from turning brown during cooking.

2. Place artichokes in a deep, heavy pot and cover them with water. Toss in all spices and garlic, then cook, partially covered, at a gentle boil until leaves pull away easily. This will take about 40 minutes.

3. Remove artichokes from water, leaving the bits of spices clinging to them. You can serve these warm or chilled, depending on your preference. It also works to cook them in advance, then put them back into boiling water to reheat for 8 to 10 minutes.

Backbone Sauce

We really wanted a signature sauce to serve with our burger and meat loaf. We consider this an upgrade of Utah's unofficial condiment, "fry sauce"—ketchup and mayonnaise. It's delicious on a grilled burger with melted sharp white cheddar and caramelized onions, on BLTs, or as a dip for artichokes.

½ cup sour cream
1 cup mayonnaise
1 or 2 chipotle peppers (include adobo sauce, in which they're packed)
2 tablespoons cumin
2 cloves roasted garlic
1 red pepper, roasted and peeled
juice of one lime
2 tablespoons chopped cilantro
a pinch of salt and pepper

In a food processor fitted with a blade, whirl together all the ingredients. Scrape sides and process till smooth.

Pueblo Rice

A zingy, crunchy concoction created on the fly in our first year, this side dish hasn't left the menu yet—leftovers are great scrambled into eggs in the morning.

The rice:
2½ cups water
½ teaspoon salt
1 tablespoon butter
1 cup rinsed brown basmati rice

1. Bring water and salt to a boil. Stir in butter and rice. Cover.

2. Cook over very low heat until all water is absorbed, about 35 minutes. Don't lift the lid! Let stand, covered, while assembling remaining ingredients.

The rest:
¼ cup toasted piñons (pine nuts)
⅓ cup toasted pepitas (hulled pumpkin seeds)
roasted corn shaved from one cob
½ red bell pepper, finely chopped
⅓ cup orange juice
juice from one lime
2 tablespoons canola oil
2 teaspoons coriander
1 teaspoon salt

Whisk all ingredients together and toss with cooked rice.

Moqui Mac

As macaroni and cheese connoisseurs, we have created this, our version of cheesy baked perfection. It's the ultimate in comfort carbo loading.

2 tablespoons butter
1 onion, minced
1 tablespoon salt
1 cup roasted corn kernels
1 cup roasted poblano chiles, peeled, seeded, and chopped
1 cup roasted red peppers, peeled, seeded, and chopped
1 minced jalapeño pepper
3 cups heavy cream (or half & half or milk)
2 cups grated pepper jack cheese
2 cups chopped tomatoes with juice
1 teaspoon Dijon mustard
⅛ teaspoon each: cayenne, nutmeg
½ teaspoon each: black pepper, ground cumin
1 package (16 ounces) macaroni, cooked according to package directions
⅓ cup grated Parmesan plus ⅓ cup bread crumbs

1. In a large saucepan over medium-high heat, melt butter. Add onion and salt. When onion is soft, add corn, chiles, red peppers, and jalapeño and cook 10 minutes on medium heat.

2. Add cream and bring almost to a boil on medium heat. Cook 10 minutes.

3. Remove from heat and add cheese, tomatoes, mustard, and spices. Adjust salt to taste.

4. Heat oven to 350 degrees. Combine cheese sauce with just-cooked pasta and pour into a greased medium-sized baking dish or individual crocks. Top with Parmesan and bread crumb mixture and bake for 30 to 40 minutes, till top of casserole is crusty and edges are bubbly. Let sit 10 minutes before eating.

Piñons, also called pine nuts, are the edible seeds from the cones of the Piñon variety of pine tree that grows in the Southwestern part of the United States. Shelled piñons are highly prized for their smooth texture and sweet flavor. To bring out the taste of piñons, lightly toast them in a dry cast-iron skillet over medium heat.

Hulled green pumpkin seeds (pepitas), widely available in health food stores, add a delicious crunch to salads and rice dishes. Their use in Mexican cooking dates back to Pre-Columbian times. It's best to buy them raw and toast them yourself, either in a dry cast-iron skillet over medium heat or in a microwave. As they cook, they'll start to make a distinct popping sound. This is your cue that they're getting close. They should be a very light golden brown color and will look rounder than when they were raw.

Flowers

To create a little flower is the labor of ages.

—WILLIAM BLAKE

Our connection with flowers, much like many of our affiliations in Boulder, is both professional and poetic. Flowers play an essential role in our lives as restaurateurs. They have, in a sense, become our signature. Before we even knew each other, flowers were already quietly insinuating themselves into our culinary zones. Blake was working as a caterer and outdoor chef but had long dreamed of owning a restaurant where fresh-cut wildflowers graced every table; Jen was a professional baker, decorating all her wedding cakes with an array of colorful blossoms.

Fortunately, Boulder came with a profusion of flowers to play with, and the grill itself is engulfed with the ones we inherited or planted ourselves. They tend to be people's first impression of the restaurant—the vegetable garden at the entrance to the lodge grounds is bordered by giant sunflowers, and the grill is encircled by a wide moat of flowers: pillars of white and pink hollyhocks so tall and bright they can be seen from the highway; dark purple morning glories crawling high up the wall; nasturtiums trailing all over the ground. To the left of the front door there's an explosion of cosmos, and the flowers continue wrapping protectively around the restaurant: bachelor's buttons, yarrow, zinnias, roses, marigolds, alyssum, and below the redwood deck, daisies, echinacea, white and red chrysanthemums, and columbine. On both sides of the front door sit large clay pots overflowing with snapdragons, pansies, and violets. This jungle of flowers, so startlingly beautiful and fragrant, is a potent daily reminder of what crazy luck we have, owning a restaurant in such an unspoiled, uncontrived place. We believe that the smallest details often reveal the purest expressions of the heart—and these flowers are a personal symbol of our hospitality.

One of the countless advantages of keeping our gardens pesticide-free is that it enables us to garnish with edible flowers. We drop them into soups and salads, top desserts with them, and scatter them over entrées. Even drinks aren't exempt—our freshly squeezed rosemary limeade might come with a tiny violet floating in it. Edible flowers are absolutely unparalleled in their power to bring brightness, sophistication, and romance to a dish. Sprinkling delicate red and gold marigold petals over a big, macho slab of steak is like putting a tuxedo on a cowboy—the reason it's so stylish and elegant is that it's entirely unexpected.

Any discourse on edible flowers would be incomplete and wildly irresponsible without the following standard, compulsory caveat: when garnishing or cooking with flowers, never, ever (We mean it! Never!) use a flower unless you're absolutely positive it's edible. It's also wise to note that while some flowers are suitable for consumption, they may taste sharp and pungent and will quickly ruin your perfectly wonderful meal. Nor should you add flowers to your food if you're unsure of their origin. Many edible flower varieties are cultivated exclusively for use as cut flower decoration and are sprayed with potentially harmful pesticides and insecticides, which makes eating them not only regrettable but also quite dangerous.

Some of our favorite edible flowers

Nasturtium. With round, flat leaves resembling lily pads and beautiful orange, red, or yellow blossoms, nasturtiums taste peppery, like mustard or watercress. Both flower and leaf are edible: tuck the blossoms onto a plate beside your entrée and toss the leaves into a salad mix to give it a kick.

Pansy. Pansies have a grassy, vaguely sarsaparilla flavor, and the entire flower can be used to dress up hors d'oeuvres or desserts or—if your intentions veer from the purely culinary—as a love charm.

Marigold/Calendula. Marigolds' beautiful orange and gold petals taste tangy and somewhat spicy, a bit like saffron. Nip the petals and scatter them over a main dish to liven it up.

Chrysanthemum. The entire chrysanthemum flower can be consumed and makes a glorious addition to a dinner plate. Tangy and slightly bitter, it has been compared in flavor to cauliflower.

Violet. We especially love decorating our desserts with violets—against a backdrop of freshly whipped cream, the deep, rich color of a tiny violet is radiant and inviting. Violets can be eaten whole—they have a subtle, sweet flavor.

Borage. Borage has lovely blue, star-shaped flowers that lift easily off the stem and a cool, cucumber taste. Add them as garnish to salads and soups, or use them to flavor sauces.

Left to right: red heirloom rose, yellow heirloom rose, and bachelor's button.

Rose. Silky, tender rose petals add color and a touch of romance to any plate. Scatter them over salads, float them in soup, or use them to adorn desserts.

Bachelor's Button. The brilliant blue petals can be clipped and sprinkled generously onto entrées and salads as well as on the actual plate surrounding the meal. The petals look particularly stunning against a white plate.

Herbs. All herbs that flower, such as thyme, sage, oregano, and anise hyssop, are edible.

The Meaning of Flowers

Nasturtium. To the Victorians, the nasturtium signified a jest. The meaning of the word is "a twist of the nose." We didn't know this when we chose the nasturtium as part of our logo. But now we understand everything. Ah yes. A jest. Of course. Nasturtiums have also been linked to conquest, victory in battle, maternal love (this is appropriate as we are rather nauseatingly head over heels in maternal love with Helles B.), charity, and patriotism.

Bachelor's Button. The blue bachelor's button signifies hope in solitude. The name is derived from the Middle Ages in England: when a girl placed a blossom from this flower beneath her apron, she could win the heart of any bachelor she desired. It has also been associated with celibacy, though. Hmm.

Pansy. Pansies were named after the French word for thought, *penser,* and were once believed to be a charmed flower—legend has it you could hear a lover's secret thoughts in a plucked pansy. Pansies have been said to connote the unspoken yet reciprocal thoughts of lovers. They're also known as Johnny-jump-ups, love-in-idleness, call-me-to-you, three-faces-under-a-hood, godfathers and godmothers, flower o'luce, and banwort.

Marigold/Calendula. Historically valued for its medicinal and culinary uses, the marigold got its name in the Middle Ages, when early Christians called it "Mary's Gold" for its adornment of statues of the Virgin Mary. The botanical name, *calendula,* means "throughout the months." Because the marigold offers its head up to the sun year-round, it has been called summer's bride, husbandman's dial, and little lover. In the language of flowers, however, the calendula symbolizes joy and winning grace. No wonder we feel the need to feed it to people.

Chrysanthemum. The white chrysanthemum stands for truth, the red for love. Additionally, because it blooms in autumn, it suggests the glimmer of hope in darkness. An auspicious flower throughout Asia, the chrysanthemum is identified with harvest, rest, and ease. (These are a few of our favorite things . . .)

Violet. The violet represents faithfulness. Shakespeare used this dainty fleur in sonnets to suggest humility and constancy in love. It also symbolizes modesty and promises to soothe tempers and cure insomnia. A number of ailments ranging from ulcers to headaches to asthma can allegedly be cured with violets. Violets arrive in the spring hidden by heart-shaped leaves, which explains the association with modesty.

Borage. The borage flower signifies courage. (We approve of this definition, because at times it feels courageous to refrain from selling Helles to some naïve buyer from the city after convincing him or her that it's always great fun and a total snap to run a restaurant in the center of nowhere.) The Latin name, *borago,* is said to be an altered form of *corago,* meaning "I bring heart." A plant long used for medicinal purposes, it's known for its ability to support the production of adrenaline and help the body cope with stressful situations.

Yellow Rose. Yellow roses are said to symbolize friendship, beauty, home, familial love, and oh yeah! Texas.

Red Rose. No big secret here—someone who gives you red roses is hot for you. This flower is all about passion, love, romance. OK, send us some.

Chocolate Chile Cream Pots

We pretty much have to keep this unbelievably rich and luscious dessert on the menu all season long, because returning diners complain if they can't order it. It's a certain cure for any emotional ill.

>   6 large egg yolks (we use only local farm eggs for this—substitute free-range and organic store-bought)
>   9 ounces high-quality sweet chocolate
>   2 ounces high-quality unsweetened chocolate
>   2 cups heavy cream
>   ½ cup half & half
>   ½ teaspoon salt
>   2 teaspoons powdered hot Chimayo chile

1. Whip egg yolks thoroughly in a blender. Set aside. Carefully heat chocolate, cream, and half & half together in a heavy-bottomed pot, stirring constantly until chocolate is completely melted and bubbling and mixture is a very even consistency and color. Add salt and chile powder and let simmer a minute more.

2. Pour the very hot chocolate mixture into a whirling blender of egg yolks and blend until thick and completely smooth. If for any reason the custard doesn't thicken up properly, pour into a heavy-bottomed saucepan and cook it on very low heat. It may temporarily break, but another quick go in the blender will fix the problem.

3. While chocolate is still hot, pour it into dessert cups (we use small white ramekin dishes—a little bit of this dessert goes far). Chill cream pots for 1 hour.

We garnish this dessert with freshly whipped cream, grated Abuelita Mexican chocolate, and edible flower petals or a whole small, dried red chile from our garden (although one time a guest ate the chile and nearly fainted . . . now the servers warn the guests about the garnish, because it looks too pretty to skip).

Whipped Cream

Use good organic cream and fine vanilla extract. In a stand mixer with the whisk attachment combine:

>   2 cups heavy cream
>   ¼ cup powdered sugar
>   ½ teaspoon vanilla extract

Start whipping the cream on slow to give powdered sugar a chance to incorporate. Bring speed to medium for a few minutes, until cream resembles fluffy clouds.

Overmixed cream turns to chunky sweet yellow butter, which could be nice on French toast. Do NOT serve cream that has passed into the butter realm.

A delicious option for topping fruit desserts is maple whipped cream: omit sugar and vanilla then whip the cream with ¼ cup maple syrup.

Lemon Chiffon Cake

We love this cake. Our customers love this cake. It was featured in *O, The Oprah Magazine,* which we also love. Make it and be happy.

The cake:
2 cups flour
1½ cups sugar
1 tablespoon baking powder
1 teaspoon salt
1 cup cold water
7 egg yolks
8 egg whites
½ cup canola oil
2 teaspoons vanilla extract
zest from 2 lemons
½ teaspoon cream of tartar

The icing:
⅓ cup softened (not melted) butter
2 cups powdered sugar
3 teaspoons lemon juice

1. Preheat oven to 335 degrees. In a large bowl, combine flour, sugar, baking powder, and salt.

2. In a small bowl, throughly combine water, yolks, oil, vanilla, and zest. Stir yolk mixture into dry ingredients until smooth.

3. In a large mixing bowl, beat egg whites with cream of tartar at medium-low speed until foamy and frothy. Increase speed and beat whites until stiff, but not dry, peaks.

4. Pour yolk mixture over whites in ribbons, folding mixtures together very gently until just combined. Pour into ungreased 10" tube pan.

5. Bake 55 minutes at 350 degrees until the top springs back when touched. Immediately invert pan and hang upside down on the neck of a bottle for 2 hours to cool.

6. Run a long, thin knife around the edge of the pan to loosen cake and remove from pan. The wider end of the cake will be the top.

7. Make icing by combining all ingredients in small mixing bowl and whipping until smooth. Spread icing over cake top, allowing some to drip over the sides.

License to Serve

Utah is known far and wide for its somewhat unusual and strict liquor laws. Having visited before we moved here, we imagined ourselves reasonably conversant with the intricacies involved in getting a drink in the Beehive (or "Behave") State. We knew it was complicated, but boy, were we in for an education.

When we arrived in Boulder in the year 2000 to open our restaurant, statewide and local laws prevented us from serving any type of alcohol. The Boulder town council, all of whose members were Mormon, had routinely denied all past restaurant owners the right to apply for a liquor license. The two convenience stores in town were allowed to sell 3.2 percent beer, but no restaurant in Boulder history had ever served alcohol.

With a restaurant supported principally by tourism, we knew the absence of a liquor license would sting, and it did. Our customers came to us having scaled sandstone slickrock, crawled through canyons, and pulled cactus spines out of their ankles all day. Their throats were parched and full of red dust, and they wanted beer and they wanted it now. Most of our dinner guests felt, at the very least, inconvenienced and irritated by the situation—many associated alcohol with elegant dining—but for a lot of the tourists, it was an outright abomination. The Germans thought it odd and the French found it positively uncivilized. Blake stood tableside night after night, patiently trying to explain that in certain ways, Boulder was very much like a foreign country itself, and wouldn't it be friendlier if they approached the liquor situation from that point of view? Sometimes this worked; often it didn't. As a method of stalling it was good, but what we really needed was a wine list.

Newcomers to any small town are bound to meet resistance trying to modify long-standing regulations, but our case seemed especially foredoomed. The people of this particular town were not only predominantly nondrinkers, they had also recently been authorized by the state to defend local liquor laws and were resolute about continuing to do so. The town council had just resolved a lawsuit in which Boulder restaurant owners requested and were refused the right to apply for a liquor license. The case went all the way to the Utah Supreme Court before the town of Boulder finally won. The state handed back a decision saying that the town had the right to withhold local consent—in other words, deny permission to apply for the license.

For us, securing a liquor license was simply a crucial component in making our restaurant a profitable business. At our second town meeting, shortly after we opened, the alcohol permit issue came up. We recognized the subject as a source of conflict but put a positive face forward and appealed to their business sensibilities. We didn't view having a permit as some sort of inherent right, we explained to the council. Rather, we hoped that if the town ever allowed us to apply for a license, the move would come as an expression of the will of the people, with the understanding that the permit was necessary for our economic success.

The next day, one of the town council members stopped by the restaurant. He said, "No one ever presented the alcohol permit from a financial perspective before—that's something we can all understand. You've cast the issue in a new light."

At that point we crossed our fingers, held our collective breath, and continued to work, listening to customers tell us they were pretty sure our food would taste better with beer or wine. We served them herbal sun tea and fresh-squeezed rosemary limeade, as well as eight fancy fizzy drinks we used as decoys to take their minds off the Chardonnay. We were trying. And we showed up at town meetings, hired locals to work for us, and just generally did our best to prove that we wanted to become contributing members of the community, that we were intent on helping Boulder grow in a responsible way. Finally, after two years, the mayor (also the church bishop) announced that he felt it was time for the town to vote on the liquor license issue.

We could hardly believe it when a majority of the town's population voted in favor of granting local restaurants the right to apply for liquor licenses. This was huge. We were thrilled and humbled. Unfortunately, it was only the first of many hurdles. We still had to apply at the state level, which meant mountains of paperwork, fingerprinting, an FBI background check, and a presentation before the Utah Department of Alcohol and Beverage Control (DABC) board in Salt Lake City. We presented our case to the DABC along with fourteen other restaurants from all over Utah, also vying for one of three licenses being issued. When the state granted us the first liquor license in the history of the town, we were overwhelmed, excited, and profoundly relieved. We were also completely unprepared and had to make a beer run to Hills and Hollows, our local convenience store, to buy six-packs to serve that night. In Utah, all draft beer is 3.2 percent (alcohol by volume), as opposed to the standard 6 percent beer served in most other states. "Heavy" beer is available in some parts of Utah, but only bottled.

We were given a full liquor license, but in deference to the wishes of the town council, we choose to serve only beer and wine. Doing so also corresponds with our philosophy of serving regionally based foods and drinks. We sell Utah beer and California and Pacific Northwest wine, but it's not as easy as it sounds. We drive nine hours round-trip to Salt Lake City to fetch our wine, and whatever we sell must be purchased through the DABC. We can supply corkage on wine that customers bring, but only if the bottle bears a DABC sticker proving it was purchased in Utah. All the beers we serve are microbrews, delivered to us in kegs from Wasatch Brewery.

It really wouldn't be a gross exaggeration to say obtaining the liquor license was Helles's salvation—and in some ways, our own. "After we got our license," Blake says, "I realized that it had been the hardest part of my job—explaining to people every night why we didn't serve alcohol and convincing them that they were happy about it." Even more important to us, however, it now serves as a symbol of the community's willingness to embrace us as a viable business.

We send all our staff through liquor law training, instructed by the compliance division of the DABC, and adhere to the DABC's involved list of rules. (A few examples: Servers are required to wear a name tag or number at all times to make them identifiable by undercover compliance officers; only five ounces of wine can be poured at a time; alcohol must be kept under lock and key between the hours of midnight and noon; underage servers cannot discuss alcohol with customers; and alcohol cannot be served in a restaurant unless the customer also orders or at least expresses the intention to order food.)

Many of our servers at the grill are Mormon, and though they serve wine, they never drink it. A few times a year our gifted wine broker, Tracey Thompson, comes down from Salt Lake City to educate our staff and hold wine tastings for us in the dining room. For our LDS employees she holds wine sniffings. Sniffings are a routine part of Tracey's job, as she teaches about wine to restaurant employees all over Utah, a great many of whom are LDS. "I actually really enjoyed learning about wine," says Joseph Barsch, one of our LDS servers. "We weren't serving hard alcohol, which I appreciate—I've never had to deal with anyone going over the edge. But I've always had a love for class and culture; I enjoy the smell of fine tobacco as much as anyone else. Of course, I never drink, but I enjoy the ceremony of taking a bottle of wine to the table and opening it. It's a skill—I had no idea about wines or anything else like that, and I still have a huge amount to learn, but I feel like in the future it could serve me in good stead. I don't mind it, not at all."

In 2002, Hell's Backbone Grill became the first restaurant in the history of Boulder, Utah, to receive a liquor license. Today the restaurant presents a thoughtfully selected wine list and serves a handful of Utah draft beers from Wasatch Brewery, including Polygamy Porter and St. Provo Girl Pilsner.

Dinner's Finest Complement

Wine is bottled poetry.

—ROBERT LOUIS STEVENSON

We thoughtfully select each bottle we serve, choosing wines that meet three very essential requirements: First and foremost, we purchase wines that taste good to us and that bring out the flavor of our dishes; these are wines we drink ourselves and offer to our family and friends. Second, wines produced by vineyards committed to sustainable agricultural practices, and third, wines with pretty labels. We *are* girls, after all.

Our list is lovingly created and includes a small and interesting selection of different varietals. We aim to offer an imaginative assortment, but our choices in wine reflect our value system. Therefore, we stock only wines from the Pacific Northwest and California, the major viticultural regions closest to Utah. We've been pleased to find that many of these vineyards are committed to sustainable agriculture and organic farming; wineries producing unique, elegant vintages with a sense of place and a profound connection to the land.

"Blake and Jen design their wine menu," says Tracey Thompson, our wine consultant, "as an extension of their food menu and their vision. Over the years I've made recommendations to them, and they invariably repeat the same criteria—organic, close to home, and mindfully produced. Their commitment to the land is an inextricable part of how they express themselves through food and wine."

We love a lot of winemakers but have three special favorites. Robert Sinskey Vineyard and Alma Rosa Winery & Vineyards are both certified organic. These wines appear on our list more than once, not only for their incredible complexity and food-pairing abilities but also because we respect the integrity, originality, and principles of these winemakers. And not incidentally, because we completely love the way they taste. The third,

Bonny Doon Vineyard, we adore because they're committed to farming conscientiously with minimal processing, they offer innovative and progressive approaches to winemaking, and their weird and wacky humor shows up in their labels, never failing to amuse us. Basically, they're as clever and funny as we aspire to be. And their wines are freakin' delicious.

The Soundtrack

If music be the food of love, play on.

—WILLIAM SHAKESPEARE

Our music mix is a highly scientific, emotionally charged formula concisely detailed in the form of a note taped to the stereo. The formula involves a mix of mellow jazz (nothing "squonky"), oldies, bluegrass, nice acoustic singer-songwriter types, and music from faraway places. Classical we love to play in the morning, but always the entire disk—never in a mix. It's the flavor of the restaurant, we tell our employees, not a chance to play their personal music. Not a chance for self-expression. Not an appropriate time for angst guitar. Because if the music is wrong then the mood can't be right.

Our Top-Twentyish Playlist:

1. The Noble Jones Project—*Synergy*
2. Onus B. Johnson—*Box of Moonlight*
3. Alison Krauss
4. The Be Good Tanyas—*Blue Horse* and *Chinatown*
5. Salamander Crossing—*Henry Street, a Retrospective*
6. Tim and Molly O'Brien—*Away Out On The Mountain*
7. Dolly Parton
8. Iris Dement—*Infamous Angel*
9. Hot Club of Cowtown—*Dev'lish Mary*
10. Loretta Lynn
11. Jack Johnson—*Brushfire Fairytales*
12. David Gray—*White Ladder*
13. Lyle Lovett (Any and all. Lyle, if you are reading this, please report to the kitchen.)
14. Marty Robbins
15. Nancy Griffith
16. The soundtrack from the movie *Big Night*
17. Bill Frisell—*Nashville*
18. Katherine Whalen's Jazz Squad
19. Robinella and the CC String Band
20. Ry Cooder and Ali Farka Toure—*Talking Timbuktu*
21. Gillian Welch—*Soul Journey*
22. Yonder Mountain String Band

From the Garden

Organic gardening is a method of agriculture that relies wholly on the earth's natural resources—pests and weeds are managed using earth-friendly means; natural nutrients and products such as leaves, manure, and composted food are built into the soil to fertilize plants without the use of chemicals; and artificial products such as petroleum-based fertilizers, herbicides, and pesticides are strictly avoided. Essentially, everything used in the garden to promote healthy plant growth comes from the earth itself and won't pollute, harm, or imbalance the environment, contaminate the water supply, or hurt beneficial organisms.

Anna Kellerman, our primary gardener, worked on three organic farms in New York before coming to work for us. "Blake and Jen's mission here is great," Anna says. "They value the integrity of food—fresh, organic food. Locally grown produce is important for the effect it has on the environment, and it tastes better when it's not coming from thousands of miles away. People staying at the lodge always see me working in the garden and ask, 'Is that for the restaurant, for our dinner?' They comment on how beautiful it is: 'What are you picking? Is that Swiss chard?' I like playing the role of food-bringer. When I'm walking from the garden with a big bowl of string beans or tomatoes, I feel really good, like my job has importance, and I'm doing something in line with nature and the seasons—knowing the food is going to benefit so many people I don't even know. At that moment, bringing all that food feels very fulfilling."

While the rewards of organic gardening are boundless and multifarious, it's nevertheless a method of farming that requires work, commitment, patience, and creativity. And because of our fussy, unpredictable high-desert weather, our remote location, and restaurant ethos, there exists for us a host of additional complexities. We are constantly learning and experimenting, discovering with each new season what works and doesn't in this climate and at our elevation, what methods are suitable and effective, what supplies are available, and what corresponds with our belief system. It's like a never-ending research project, one that comes complete with nasty sunburns, dirty fingernails, ant bites, frosts, ruined crops, humbling mistakes, surprise bonanzas, great and tiny victories, and, in the end, the proud pleasure of gathering beautiful, homegrown, brightly colored vegetables and filling up your stomach with them.

Ana Rendón at work in the lettuce patch.

"One of my main challenges," says Anna, "was coming from the Northeast where rain does a lot of the watering for you. Here we get very little rain, so we rely heavily on flood irrigation, which maximizes the water." We dig channels through our garden, a traditional style of watering used by early settlers. When the plants are small we use top water, and as soon as they're established, we flood the garden for half an hour every other day, except in the summer, when we do it every day.

We may not get much rain in Boulder, but we see more than our share of snow. Therefore, in the winter we cover or "overwinter" our gardens. Though a long and arduous process, this allows us to harvest some vegetables in the spring when we open the restaurant—hardy veggies like carrots that have survived the winter under a thick covering of mulch.

Another major challenge for us is the pursuit of supplies. Living so far from everything, this is a tough task. We have no nursery nearby, which means all supplies must be mail-ordered or picked up by someone coming in from out of town.

From the Gardener

○ Normal fertilizers are usually chemicals synthesized in a lab, which leach right into the groundwater, contaminating it. Organic fertilizer, made of nitrogen-rich fish emulsion and kelp, can be ordered from Planet Natural. It's also helpful in transplanting—dip the plant roots in the liquid fertilizer before putting them in the soil. In the past, Native Americans would sometimes put a dead fish in with the plant to lend the soil nitrogen and necessary nutrients. Another easy, natural fertilizer can be made from compost or manure. Brew a "tea" of compost or manure and spray the leaves of plants with it.

○ When starting seeds in flats, you need a sterile medium. Seedlings are susceptible to disease, so it's best to avoid using compost or recycled soil. You can make a seed-starting mix out of peat moss, vermiculite, and perlite, then once a week, spray with a fish emulsion organic fertilizer.

○ Lettuce wilts in the middle of the day and tastes bitter in the afternoon, so we harvest it only in the early morning.

○ When eating organically and "earth to table," you won't worry about ingesting pesticides; however, it's still important to wash everything really well, especially lettuce—otherwise you might find happy little green worms in your salad. Other frequent unwanted visitors are earwigs, which commonly live in nasturtiums. If you find one, squeeze the flower and it will pop right out. (Best you do this outside and not at the dinner table.)

"The funniest thing that happens to me," Jen says, "is when I make this lovely plate with food from the garden, fresh herbs, just-picked garnish, fruit, and flowers. Then I hear about the earwig or spider or worm that crawled over the chicken breast. How embarrassing! But then I think, at least they know it's fresh! It's the same with eggshells or lemon seeds: at least you know it's homemade."

Then there's the composting issue. Composting is a technique of mixing decayed organic matter to use in fertilizing plants. It also helps suppress weeds, prevent plant disease, and conserve water. It's a key component of organic gardening and isn't difficult to do on your own. The thing is, as a restaurant we generate so much compost, our gardeners find themselves with far more than they know what to do with. We collect about four buckets of kitchen and table scraps a day—in four separate buckets, for four reasons—one for eggshells, one for onion skins, one for regular compost, and one to feed our friend Gloria's pig. We're also fortunate enough to have wonderful neighbors who are more than happy to hand over their compost gold, also known as farm animal dung. They graciously provide us with all the cow, horse, and llama manure we require. "The problem is finding someone to help turn the compost," says Anna. "I have a local boy now who comes once a week. But we're producing so much, I'm running out of room!"

The most complicated aspect of gardening we face is pest control. While many organic practices entail finding alternate, earth-friendly ways to kill pests, because of the Buddhist thing, we don't kill any insects. We try to relocate them instead, which is ultimately better for us but not exactly a pleasurable way to spend the afternoon. Seriously—it's no picnic moving an anthill. Nevertheless, it's our preferred method of managing insects. But it's not everyone's. Understandable.

With that in mind, here are a few additional natural, compassionate ideas on pest control from our lovely and talented gardener, Anna:

Introduce beneficial insects into the garden. To deter aphids, for example, two thousand ladybugs can be ordered inexpensively from Planet Natural and FedExed to you in a muslin bag with directions. (Wasps and beetles are also available.)

Companion planting is a reliable, organic solution to pest control. Nasturtiums, marigolds, mint, basil, chives, and chrysanthemums all repel bugs without harming them. Interplant lettuce with your carrots, onions with your tomatoes, potatoes with your cabbage, and beans with your corn to steer mischievous insects in another direction.

Homemade garlic-pepper sprays make an effective bug deterrent. Combine one teaspoon garlic, one teaspoon black pepper, and one cup water. Increase the quantities to make a gallon and brew by cooking it on medium heat for twenty minutes. (Don't let it boil.) Transfer it into a bottle and spray the plant leaves.

The garden behind Blake's house is our principal producer. It's top-watered using water from the original irrigation system designed by the settlers of Boulder.

Summer

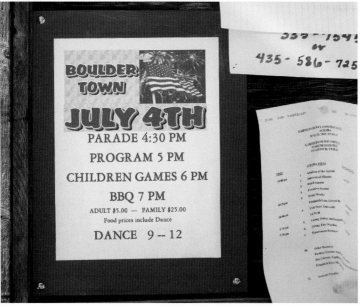

Summer

Summer afternoon—Summer afternoon...
the two most beautiful words in the
English language.

—HENRY JAMES

Summertime in Boulder, compared to the rest of southern Utah, is pleasantly temperate due to its high elevation. Occasionally it gets hot, but even then monsoon rains cool everything off and turn the nights clear and the mornings bright. When we first opened the restaurant, summer was our slow season. So to attract customers and keep ourselves from being bored out of our minds, we began holding community events at the restaurant—ice cream socials and talent shows and bluegrass festivals and other activities of that ilk. What started out as distractions have since become community traditions, and although we're now as busy as ever in the summer and have enough to do running the restaurant, we can't resist the excuse to throw a party or five—especially when the whole town's expecting us to do so.

Fourth of July in Boulder is a sweet, small-town affair. The parade, which takes approximately four and a half minutes to watch, circles the town center—about six blocks total—on horses and in fire trucks and the odd horse-drawn carriage, not to mention plenty of pickup trucks carrying enthusiastic local kids with water guns. We participate each year by hula-hooping the entire way. We recruit a team made up of restaurant staff and their kids, practice some tricks, and proceed with our custom hand-painted and cloth-covered hula hoops down the road. Team Hula we call ourselves and yes, we are an absolutely magnificent spectacle of impressive talent.

In the past few years, we've established several new summertime Boulder traditions, including the annual talent show and Folksfest. The talent show started as an utter fluke—due to hazardous forest conditions, fireworks were unexpectedly canceled one year. So along with the lodge, we threw a talent show together at the last minute. It was an enormous success—most of the town showed up and the acts were, and continue to be, amazing and varied—juggling, storytelling, ballroom dancing, bandana tricks, and cowboy poetry.

At summer's end we work with the lodge to host Folksfest, a two-day concert festival featuring local and out-of-town country, bluegrass, and folk bands. Also a farmers market,

it's an opportunity for Boulder locals to sell handmade and homegrown wares, such as wood carvings, garden produce, and homemade vinegars. One hundred percent of the gate proceeds go back to the town to help support a local conservation easement for a public park. And Dave Mock, the lodge owner, always donates money as well as matching the gate. Folksfest generates publicity for the town and raises money to create a lovely public space for locals and visitors. We love Folksfest because it's a very tangible way to give back to the community. Also, since we're so far away from concert venues, we think it's a pretty ingenious way to bring the bands to us.

Aside from throwing parties, our other preoccupation in summer is the garden. We tend to get all our crops at once, so the kitchen becomes a whirlwind of preserving. Our peak harvest falls between July and October, when we get beans (both pole and bush), beets, summer squashes, kale, Swiss chard, Navajo watermelon, and three kinds of carrots. The warm weather typically means a wealth of leafy green herbs and southwestern delights, such as tomatillos, jalapeños, and chile pequins.

A typical summer menu might include a porterhouse pork chop with Boulder apricot barbecue sauce, served with savory corn custard and steamed organic garden vegetables. On the small-plates menu, jalapeño and avocado cream soup, and for dessert, white chocolate and Capitol Reef apricot fool.

Clockwise from top: Local schoolteacher Stacy Davis, one of the restaurant's veteran servers, helps Blake sort out the evening's reservations. Restaurant gardener Anna Kellerman harvests lettuce, arugula, and edible flowers daily throughout the summer. Blake and Tsangpo, a Tibetan monk, enjoy a group excursion to Red Canyon, off the historic Burr Trail.

Cowboy with a Spin

When the sun rises I go to work, when the sun goes down, I take my rest, I dig the well from which I drink, I farm the soil that yields my food, I share creation. Kings can do no more.

—UNKNOWN CHINESE AUTHOR (2500 BC)

"The most important thing about this restaurant is the way people treat each other," says Joseph Barsch. "No matter who you are, if you do your job and work cheerfully and well, you're accepted. You can be a long-haired hippie, or you can be a straightlaced Mormon boy—which I don't claim to be. Well, I'm a good Mormon boy, but I'm not your typical suit-and-tie, aspiring-businessman, college-missionary type. But I do live the standards."

Joseph (pronounced Yosef) isn't typical anything—he single-handedly redefines the standard concept of a Utah Mormon rancher. He's twenty-eight years old and so versatile he's nearly impossible to classify—though attempting might prove an entertaining diversion, so here we go. Joseph is: Mormon returned missionary, rancher, writer, country boy, academic, saddle maker, artist (he tools leather), hunting guide, competitive ballroom dancer, and darned fine waiter.

He sums it up somewhat more concisely: "I'm an aspiring writer who works with my hands in doing odd jobs to get by while I try to get published." Joseph studies English with an emphasis on creative writing at Brigham Young University. He's a member of the university competitive ballroom dance team; he favors international standard ballroom dancing, which includes tango, waltz, foxtrot, and quickstep. "I had a dance instructor at the university," he says, laughing, "who always told me I was the strangest dancer he'd ever known, because you don't find anybody who shows up, pulls off his cowboy boots, and puts on Latin dance shoes."

When he was eleven, Joseph and his family moved to Boulder from the Provo area, where his Austrian father taught art at Brigham Young University. Today he shares an organic, sustainable-lifestyle farm and ranch with his father and identical twin brother, Aram. It's Old World—style ranching—the use of electricity is limited and draft horses plow the fields. The Barsches avoid modern machinery as much as possible. But despite the fact that he's spent more than half his life ranching and can usually be seen wearing a western hat, boots, jeans, and a big shiny belt buckle, Joseph resists the "cowboy" label.

"There are three kinds of cowboys," he explains. "Rodeo cowboys, drugstore rhinestone cowboys, and then the real cowboys who don't always necessarily look like cowboys, but know cattle. They know horses and they know range country—and that's kind of what I grew up with. In New York City, you see a cowboy and most likely he's never been on a horse. I try to avoid that kind of connotation."

Joseph's first experience with restaurant work has been with us; nevertheless, he's handled it with marvelous ease, demonstrating each day how unfalteringly courteous, eager, and adaptable he is. "It's been a really good place to work," he says. "There's an emphasis on quality that I appreciate—that's something I was raised with and which I've always lived with. I've never believed in producing an inferior product, whether it's service, food, saddles, anything. But the people are 90 percent of it. One of the reasons Buddhism has worked here is that it seems to me that one of its attributes is a respect for life and for other people, no matter what they are or what they believe. A lot of people are intolerant of Mormons for one reason or another, but Blake and Jen have enough respect for the people in Boulder that they've tried to fit in, rather than shape their surroundings to them. For example, when I first talked to Blake about a job here, I told her that part of the Mormon religion is that we don't believe in working on a Sabbath—that's a very holy day for us, and she said, 'You don't even need to ask for that. I would never ask an LDS person to go against their beliefs.' I really appreciated that—it was a wonderful thing for me. I've never had to worry about it.

"If I were asked to describe why this restaurant works as well as it does, it'd be pretty easy—it just takes one word, and that's *love*. I think Blake and Jen kind of set the standard for it because everybody makes mistakes, but they're good at forgiving and appreciating the people they work with. It's an interesting thing—it's hard to find that in bosses. They might value what you do, but you don't feel like they love you for it."

Top: Local twins Joseph and Aram Barsch both work as servers at the grill as well as run their own custom saddlery business. Bottom: Joseph hand-tools our menu covers. Each Hell's Backbone Grill menu is unique and skillfully crafted by Joseph and Aram.

Rosemary Limeade

People go crazy for this stuff. It's sparky, quite delicious, and a natural mixer for margaritas! On slow nights we keep our dishwashers busy squeezing limes and freezing the juice for later. We use an old manual squeezer from Mexico and juice an entire case at a time.

    4 cups simple syrup (recipe follows)
    4 cups fresh lime juice
    10 cups water

Stir it up and ice it down. Looks lovely garnished with lime rounds and small sprigs of rosemary. Makes about a gallon.

Simple Syrup:
    4 cups water
    4 cups sugar
    1 stem fresh rosemary

Combine water and sugar in saucepan. Bring to boil, stirring as sugar dissolves. Boil undisturbed and uncovered for 10 minutes. Remove from heat, add rosemary, and let mixture steep, covered, for 1 hour. You'll need the hour to squeeze limes!

Arugula Pesto

During the summer, arugula takes over our garden. We view it as an invasive yet tasty weed and use as much of it as possible by grinding it into an aromatic and intense pesto, which we freeze in case of an emergency pasta-sauce shortage.

    ½ pound arugula
    1½ tablespoons salt
    1 tablespoon brown sugar or honey
    1 tablespoon red wine vinegar
    4 roasted red peppers
    1 cup toasted piñons (pine nuts)
    1 cup toasted pepitas (hulled pumpkin seeds)
    1 cup olive oil

Blend everything together in a food processor, stopping to scrape sides and processing again. We like the pesto rich, salty, and oily. A few cloves of sweet roasted garlic are a nice addition.

Older arugula can be bitter; for a milder flavor replace half the arugula with fresh spinach leaves.

Spread on pizza crust and top with cheese and veggies; toss with hot pasta (ziti is a particularly good vehicle); add to sour cream for a dip. You can freeze the pesto in greased ice cube trays for easy-access portions.

Backbone House Salad

Salt Lake Magazine recognized this salad as one of the best in the state, and it's easily our most requested recipe. We top our salad with seasonal fruit from local orchards. In early spring, we order strawberries from our suppliers until our own are ready to harvest. As always, the freshest, locally grown, organic ingredients make a world of difference. Build the salad on individual plates in the order the ingredients are listed. Drizzle with our house honey-chile dressing.

romaine hearts, torn into small pieces
garden spring mix
jicama, sliced into matchstick-sized bits
toasted pepitas (hulled pumpkin seeds)
super-sweet dehydrated corn *[handwritten: grilled corn]*
sliced fresh fruit: strawberries, cherries,
    plums, raspberries, peaches, pears,
    or apricots

Honey-Chile Dressing

½ cup red wine vinegar
¼ cup honey
¾ teaspoon ground star anise
¼ teaspoon Dijon mustard
I teaspoon Chimayo red chile powder
¼ teaspoon salt
I cup canola oil

Combine all ingredients except oil in a blender. With machine running, slowly dribble in oil. Whirl a minute to combine. This dressing will keep for 10 days in the refrigerator.

Jicama and Red Pepper Haystacks

Refreshing, light, and easy to prepare, this salad makes a perfect summer side dish.

I small jicama (about I pound)
2 red bell peppers (cucumber or melon
    could be a delicious alternative or
    addition).
juice and zest of 2 limes
juice of I orange
I jalapeño pepper, seeded and very finely
    diced, or ½ teaspoon crushed red
    pepper flakes
salt to taste

Peel jicama and cut into matchsticks. (Hey, it kinda looks like hay!) Remove seeds and membranes from red bell peppers and cut into smaller matchsticks. Toss everything together and adjust lime and salt to suit your taste. Refrigerate salad until thoroughly chilled or serve right away.

The Monks of Drepung Loseling

If you knew what I know about the power of giving, you would not let a single meal pass without sharing it in some way.

—BUDDHA

Every summer a group of ten Tibetan monks from the Drepung Loseling Monastery come to visit Boulder for a week. The monastery, first established near Lhasa, Tibet, in 1416, was for nearly six hundred years the largest and most prestigious monastery in Tibet and, with ten thousand monks living in it, the largest monastic institution in the world. With the communist Chinese invasion of Tibet in 1959, the monastery was closed. Later, a replica of the monastery was built in India. Nearly three thousand monks reside there today. Every six months, a different group of ten monks is chosen to go on tour to perform traditional Tibetan arts while heightening awareness of the human rights violations plaguing Tibet. The monks have visited over one hundred cities in the United States, been given the keys to more than a dozen cities, and were made honorary goodwill ambassadors by President Clinton.

When they come to Boulder, the lodge provides rooms for them, and we serve them Tibetan-style meals. It's also a tradition for some of the townsfolk to host them for dinner in their homes. At the end of the week the monks perform sacred temple chants and dances on the lawn for locals and visitors. Their music is internationally renowned. They have performed at Carnegie Hall and Lincoln Center and have, over the years, performed with well-known musicians such as Paul Simon, Philip Glass, Natalie Merchant, and Patti Smith. Their unique Tibetan multiphonic chanting known as *zokkay* (low tone) and *barda* (high tone) is a style of singing in which each monk simultaneously intones three notes to create a complete chord. The monks also play a variety of instruments such as ten-foot-long *dungchen* trumpets, drums, bells, cymbals, and *gyaling* horns. The dramatic combination of music, dance, and elaborate dress is absolutely mesmerizing—it's an unforgettable experience for everyone, but especially for the local children, otherwise seldom exposed to cultural events of this kind.

Drepung Loseling Monastery monks chant in an acoustically pleasing slot canyon near Boulder.

"There's a lot of things you can do when the monks are here," says Emili Holladay, eight years old. "You can play freeze tag with them. They have a costume of a snow leopard and a costume of a yak with a big head, and they come and scare us when they do the yak dance. It's really fun."

Everything seems to shift a little during the week the monks are in town—they are beautiful, kind, impossibly merry, and it's infectious. The atmosphere changes, becomes more reverential, joyful. Outside the wraparound restaurant windows, young Tibetan lamas kick a soccer ball around the lawn in their maroon robes, while others wander quietly or pile into cars with us to go shopping at Hills and Hollows convenience store or hiking at Calf Creek. The restaurant buzzes with activity and color. And while one would expect them to be reserved or bashful, they're anything but. They happily infiltrate our small kitchen, always at least two if not six of them volunteering to chop, wash, steam, and fry, dressed in our aprons, teaching us Tibetan words, telling us stories about cooking rice in their monastery for three thousand monks every day. We get to chat with them, hear their names again, look at their faces up close. And they're the ideal kitchen help, moving efficiently and gracefully, smiling and laughing a lot, acutely aware of their space.

When the monks are in town, we offer them Tibetan-style food. There is *desi,* the traditional greeting meal of saffron rice with yellow raisins and sweet potatoes; aromatic *tukpas,* or soups, with floating homemade noodles; butter tea, a black tea topped with a froth of melted butter, milk, and salt; and, of course, the *momo,* a Tibetan celebratory food. Momos are steamed, hand-formed dumplings stuffed with potato, cabbage, and minced beef or lamb. Their edges can be braided prettily or pinched to resemble flowers or crescent moons, and the flavor, especially when prepared lovingly by a band of smiling monks, is incomparable.

We feed the monks three meals a day, all family-style but with a small ceremony, serving the *geshe* (head of the participating monks) first. The result is that we work triple shifts for a week—cooking for them while running the normal restaurant meal service. It's exhausting and wonderful. They perform elaborate blessings on the restaurant and our homes, accompany us on cherry-picking expeditions, pose happily for endless photos, hike with us and chant at the bottom of red slot canyons, and, at the end of their stay, give us—and all our staff—protection cord necklaces personally blessed by the Dalai Lama. When they drive away after a week, things are different. They leave behind a deepened, almost palpable feeling of openheartedness and loving kindness, a conspicuous hum of what the Tibetans call *dekyi*—happy, blissful energy.

Top and bottom left: The monks of Drepung Loseling Monastery meet the llamas and Harleys of Boulder. Top and bottom right: Shadrup, a Tibetan friend and cook, shares the kitchen with the monks and teaches BJ how to make and form *momos,* traditional Tibetan dumplings.

Tibetan Butter Tea

It's traditional to serve this tea in the morning or upon the arrival of guests who have made a difficult journey. For service to a high lama, present it in a beautiful teacup with a lid.

1 tablespoon loose tea leaves (preferably a smoky black tea)
¼ cup half & half
1 tablespoon butter
salt

Boil tea in 4 cups water for approximately 10 minutes. Remove from flame.

Remove tea leaves from liquid by pouring through a sieve. Add half & half and butter to strained tea. Add salt to taste. (Tibetans like it very salty!) Because this will cool the tea, warm it briefly over a low flame, making sure the tea doesn't boil. For a frothy tea, pour it back and forth between two containers a few times or quickly swirl it in a blender.

Desi (Sweet Buttered Tibetan Rice)

This rice dish is served ceremonially, to celebrate auspicious occasions, such as the arrival of a teacher or the Tibetan New Year. Desi is served in individual small bowls, mounded up high to signify prosperity and abundance. When the monks arrive in Boulder, we make sure to have enough desi to serve a bowlful to everyone present.

2 cups rinsed basmati rice
4 cups water
¼ cup butter
¼ teaspoon saffron threads
½ cup golden raisins
¼ cup sugar
2 teaspoons salt

Combine rice in a heavy-bottomed saucepan with 4 cups water. Bring to a boil, give it one stir, then lower heat and cover pot. Let the rice cook for about 20 minutes or until water is absorbed.

While rice is cooking, combine saffron threads, ⅓ cup boiling water, and butter in a bowl. Stir saffron around until threads give water and butter an intense yellow color. Set aside. Meanwhile, soak raisins in cold water for 10 minutes. When rice has finished cooking, stir in saffron mixture, drained raisins, sugar, and salt. Add more salt or butter to taste.

Salt of the Earth

Nothing is more useful than the sun and salt.

—SPANISH PROVERB

W e love salt. We stand behind every individual's right to salt liberally. We're especially supportive when it's unrefined, natural salt that's never been bleached or heat-processed; is free of chemicals, additives, and anti-caking agents; and is pink, our favorite color.

We never imagined we could love salt more than we already did. Then we discovered Redmond RealSalt, one of Utah's little-known treasures. Mined nearby us in the town of Redmond, this is no ordinary salt. It's left over from one hundred and fifty million years ago, when a vast, shallow sea lay where North America is today. When this sea evaporated, it left behind an intricate network of salt deposits. Volcanoes later erupted, thoughtfully supplying thick, protective ash beds that insulated the earth against the pollutants man would later introduce.

RealSalt's distinctive hue—pink with dark reddish-brown flakes—results from a rich palette of trace minerals. Most table salts are harshly bleached and refined before packaging, which strips them of naturally occurring minerals. But RealSalt contains more than fifty minerals, including calcium, potassium, sulfur, magnesium, iron, phosphorus, manganese, copper, zinc, and iodine. The fact that no anti-caking agents are added to it is of significance as well, because according to health experts, these additives, which prevent the salt from clogging in the shaker, perform the same trick in our bodies: refined salt won't dissolve into the fluids in our system. It builds up instead, leaving dangerous deposits in organs and tissue and creating serious health problems.

RealSalt's virtues are seemingly endless. It's certified kosher. It was given the prestigious Gold Medal Taste and Best of Show award after a double-blind taste test at the American Tasting Institute. People insist it has cured their high blood pressure, arthritis, muscle pain, and fluid retention. And it is, according to us (card-carrying salt connoisseurs), the best tasting salt in America.

Considering Meat:
Compassionate Consumption

A popularly held notion is that all Buddhists are vegetarians. While it's true that certain schools of Buddhism restrict the eating of meat, in Tibetan Buddhism it's accepted. Blake's teacher, Chagdud Tulku Rinpoche, explains why in *Change of Heart.*

"We create karma no matter what we eat. It's a hopeless situation, because if we don't eat we die.

"Since we have to eat, how can we minimize the harm involved? . . . To Buddhists, every life is of equal value. Most Tibetans don't eat fish because usually several have to be consumed to satisfy a single person's hunger. Highlanders prefer to eat yak because twenty people can live on the meat of a single animal for twenty days. They often think of lowlanders as nonvirtuous because they kill so many beings when they plow the land—beings living in the ground, by exposing them to the elements and birds; beings living above the ground, by burying or squashing them; and even more beings during the cultivation and watering of crops. . . . None of these people want to create nonvirtue, but they can't avoid it. The important thing is motivation. It is highly commendable to refrain from eating meat to spare a being from suffering and death. If your intention is never to eat grains or vegetables for the same reason, that is also very good. . . .

"All beings exist interdependently. Consuming the flesh of an animal, or vegetables and grains cultivated and harvested at the expense of many insects' lives, establishes a connection with those beings. To transform that negative connection into one of virtue, . . . before a meal, we offer our food—visualizing that it multiplies to fill all of space—to the object of our faith. We dedicate the merit of our offering to everyone connected to us, including the turkey in our sandwich or the insect that died while the rice was harvested. We pray that they and all beings will have . . . the means to gain temporary and ultimate happiness. At the end of every day . . . we also dedicate our virtue. In this way, we help the beings who have died so that we may eat, live in houses, and wear clothes. . . .

"It's wonderful if you can fully uphold [the commitment not to harm]. Otherwise, assess what you can do. . . . You can always do something to reduce your negative impact and to be more helpful. Whether you decide to eat meat or remain a vegetarian, don't become self-righteous. Without condemning anyone else's lifestyle, do the best you can, remembering to offer your food and dedicate the merit to those who died so that you might live."

At the grill, we serve local beef, lamb, and pork. We believe the animals providing the meat we serve are precious beings deserving of our gratitude and prayers; therefore, prior to slaughter, each receives a dropperful of a special tincture, a blessed substance prepared by Tibetan Buddhist lamas to benefit that being in future lives. If the animal lives in Boulder, Blake will visit it to say mantras, take a photo of it, and personally administer the tincture. She then sponsors Buddhist practitioners in Asia who go into retreat for four months to pray for the animal's ultimate happiness.

The ranchers who supply our meats are all LDS members. They're aware of our sponsorship practices, and, because of their own strong religious convictions, they respect our requests for the rituals. A few of them, because they live in another town, even administer the tincture themselves.

"That was strange for me at first," admits Lynn Bown, who raises pasture-fed lambs with her husband, Paul, in Gunnison, about two hours from Boulder. "We put the tincture in the water the day before they go to slaughter—and I'm sure, the way we put it in the water trough, that our other animals have benefited from it as well—but I almost forgot the tincture this year. I couldn't find it and was in a panic. I told Paul we couldn't bring the lamb until we found it."

We also get lamb from the Barsch family. The Barsches run an organic, sustainable-lifestyle farm, using draft horses to do the majority of the work and avoiding modern machinery as much as possible.

"It's partly just for the love of the lifestyle and partly because my father always believed that was more of a proper way to treat the earth," says Joseph Barsch. The Barsches raise Navajo Churro sheep, the original breed of sheep the Navajo people kept, using no antibiotics, steroids, or shots of any kind. "What makes it organic is the way the sheep themselves are treated and the way the pastures and feed are treated," Joseph says. "We use no insecticides or fertilizers in the pastures or in the alfalfa fields. We never give them any processed, high-performance type of feed, which can include animal parts. We don't believe in that."

Blake's rituals on behalf of the lambs don't seem peculiar to Joseph. "Part of our religion—which a lot of us don't observe that much—is that we do believe animals have spirits. Everything alive has a spirit, and the way you treat them does affect your

Very Special Steak Rub

Up until now this recipe has been a heavily guarded secret.It has alchemical properties—turning meat into gold. It's particularly valuable when applied to meats like beef tenderloin, which are all about texture but not known for pronounced flavor.

4 tablespoons pasilla negro powder
2 tablespoons guajillo powder
1½ tablespoons Chimayo powder
2½ tablespoons coriander powder
2 tablespoons cumin powder
2 tablespoons turbinado or white sugar
1 tablespoon salt
2 teaspoons mustard powder
2 teaspoons black pepper
½ teaspoon thyme
2 teaspoons Mexican oregano

In a medium mixing bowl, stir together all spices.

To store: Keeps in an airtight container for several weeks. Don't contaminate the virgin rub with used steak rub. Germs. Food poisoning, possible death, and lawsuits.

Chile-Crusted Filet Mignon

Put ¼ cup rub on a plate, dredge 1½" thick filet mignon (8 to 10 ounces, patted dry) in rub, coating all surfaces. Cook steak on medium-hot preheated grill (you should be able to hold your hand 5 inches above the fire grate for 3 to 4 seconds). Grill 4 to 6 minutes on each side for a rare steak, 6 to 8 minutes for medium. Serve with poblano crema.

Poblano Crema

We love this sauce, spicy and cool, served on the side of our chile-rubbed filet. Actually, we like it as a topping for eggs, quesadillas, chicken, and just about anything else. Because the heat of fresh green chiles varies from batch to batch, add or subtract chile to adjust the temperature of the sauce to your liking.

3 poblano chiles, roasted and peeled
3 cloves peeled garlic, microwaved 20 seconds, till soft
½ cup sour cream
⅓ cup half & half
3 tablespoons chopped cilantro
4 ounces cream cheese
salt and pepper to taste

Whirl it up in the food processor, scrape sides, process again till smooth.

salvation. There's a scripture my dad likes to quote to people sometimes. To paraphrase it, the animals you come in contact with in this life will testify for or against you on the judgment day. It's rather disconcerting to some people. I've always been raised with a great respect for life. Whenever we slaughter an animal, we give a prayer of thanks and commend its soul to the Lord. With hunting it's the same thing. We always, always give thanks—first to the animal for giving its life to us, and to the Lord for blessing us with that bounty. Not all of us do this—it's probably something that those of us who were raised close to the earth do. If you're raised with animals, you know darn well they have a soul."

We buy our beef locally, from the Rockin' Winebar Ranch. Alicia and Cooter Larsen, twenty-one and twenty-two, who run the ranch, feed their cattle a grass-only diet, which results in a healthier, more flavorful meat. Grass-fed beef tends to be leaner and lower in calories than corn-fed and has higher levels of conjugated linoleic acid, a cancer-preventative agent.

"The people here in Boulder have a nature sense rather than a commercial sense," Alicia says. "They live off the land, and meat is a part of that. Worldly things aren't important here— what you wear or drive or how fancy your house is. Everyone's more down-to-earth. There's a respect in our religion for animals, other people, and the land, and raising organic beef goes hand in hand with all of it."

Sand Painting

The meat we serve is organic and clean, raised gently by our rancher friends with pride and care. In response to this, we want to do our part to make it taste extraordinary. In the case of steak, texture is paramount in distinguishing a really good cut of grilled beef from a mediocre one. Two kinds of rub exist: a wet and a dry. We use a dry rub at the restaurant because it concentrates the meat's seasonings on the outside and seals a pure beef flavor within. We created a signature dry rub consisting of eleven different ingredients. We sell it in old-fashioned quart jars; we layer the various spices, sugar, salt, and powders by color, like the desert sand paintings we were taught to make in elementary school. We're crafty that way.

Clockwise from top left: Alicia and Cooter Larsen raise the grass-fed local beef we serve at the restaurant. Locally raised, grilled-to-perfection, chile-crusted filet mignon. Aram Barsch and his family raise sheep using sustainable methods. "Desert in a Jar," our spicy, special steak rub.

Heirloom Fruit

Live each season as it passes, breathe the air, drink the drink,
taste the fruit and resign yourself to the influences of each.

—HENRY DAVID THOREAU

Out of the tall overgrowth in a field adjacent to Blake's house juts a stone pillar with a plaque designating the plot Annie's Orchard, or the Chris and Annie Hansen Memorial Orchard. The Hansens were early settlers of Boulder, and the orchard plaque describes the treacherous weeklong trip they made with their nine children from Richfield (today just two hours away on Highway 12) to Boulder. Upon arriving at their new home, the Hansens' eldest son, Franklin, wrote, "I went with father up through the orchard to the ditch where he got a bucket of water. The apricot trees were in full bloom and it was a beautiful sight."

Although Boulder was conceived as a dairy and cattle town (every pioneering Mormon city was given a charter of sorts that charged the community with its principal vocations), the growing and preserving of fruit has always been an integral part of community life as well. And what Franklin Hansen observed in 1908 holds true for us today—those apricot trees in bloom are a sight. They're also a suggestion that summer's arrived. We tend a portion of Annie's Orchard now—it's completely chemical-free and yields beautiful heirloom apricots, apples, pears, plums, grapes, and several varieties of peaches, all of which we make into preserves, jams, butters, and chutneys to use in the restaurant throughout the year.

Fruit picking has become a customary part of our lives—whatever we pick and process one season carries us through to the next. We make sour cherry barbecue sauce for pork chops or champagne-pomegranate sauce for chicken (Colleen goes every fall to Boulder City, Nevada, to pick pomegranates), apple chutney, peach cobbler, apricot fool, and strawberry-rhubarb shortcake. We feature fruit in our house salad, make dressing with it, and use it to garnish breakfast plates. In the summer, we're constantly processing fruit. We use old-fashioned recipes from the *Ball Blue Book*—we often don't remove skins, cores, or seeds. Leaving the skins and seeds adds natural pectin, a thickening agent. We cook and strain it, adding sugar and pectin as needed. It's a labor-intensive but worthwhile method. We once pitted cherries from midnight to six a.m. With our thumbs.

Capitol Reef, just an hour from us, is home to several orchards of trees constantly erupting with exquisite apples, peaches, apricots, nectarines, plums, and cherries. It's a public orchard run on the honor system: collect all you want, weigh your pickings on the scale provided, and deposit your money in the slot in the wooden box by the entrance. We're regulars and harvest throughout the picking season.

When we head out in the morning to go apricot picking, we're cheerful—it's a minor miracle that we're leaving town. A little field trip up to Torrey and we can stop in the coffee shop/bookstore on the way home. Nothing better than fruit picking followed by a double cappuccino to lift the spirits. With hats, sunglasses, and possibly bug repellent if someone's remembered, we stack a pile of empty bus tubs into the back of the car and we're off. We chatter all the way, and before we know it, we're there. The orchards supply twenty-foot ladders, and we each climb up into our own tree, picking away, humming different tunes, filling bus tub after bus tub. After bus tub. After bus tub. Up and down the trees fifteen times, filling bus tub. After bus tub.

Pounds and pounds of fat, fuzzy apricots later, we're exhausted and usually not as cheerful as before. We load up the Subaru and pile in after the fruit, a little cranky, sticking to the seat backs. We roll down the windows, scratch at bug bites. We already feel sunburned. The sun warms the fruit through the back window, and Blake cranks a Stevie Wonder CD so no one has to talk to each other. Jen gets carsick reading. Between us we've consumed two dozen apricots and cannot begin to imagine why anyone would want to eat another—whether in a dessert, in chutney, or poured over pork chops—ever again. We don't have time to go to the coffee shop/bookstore. We have exactly one hour and thirty-two minutes to drive over the mountain, unload the fruit, shower, and change before we open the restaurant for dinner.

When the fruit arrives through the back door, those who didn't go picking, didn't participate in group gluttony, and have not, therefore, sworn off apricots for the rest of their lives, have a free-for-all, filling their stomachs until they, too, can take no more. That evening or the next day, the laborious marathon of pitting, freezing, jamming, and jellying begins. We take it on like

a crusade, excesses of energy and elbow grease and all kinds of ambitious intentions. But that sort of enthusiasm can last only so long. We don't have time to process it all, so we finish one huge batch and call it a day. Or two or three. The fruit sits and we look at it. It sits and we feel bad. It sits and we work around it. It sits and looks back at us. "We have to do something about that," one of us says, referring to the sinister pile of bus tubs in the corner. "It looks bigger. Has it grown?" "Yeah . . . what are we going to do about that?" "I don't know, but we should do something about that."

Finally, Blake, the great persuader, calls Gloria and begs her to rescue us. She tells her there's a filet mignon in it for her if she'll only drag us out from under our oppressive pile of apricots. Gloria walks through the door and gets to work, and we love her even more.

And then the next month we do peaches. God help us. Next time we'll bring our own dang coffee.

Sixty Pounds of Peaches

I am in Boulder with my friends Flo and Borg, visiting my daughter Blake. It's the weekend of the bluegrass festival, and sixty pounds of peaches sit in the restaurant, waiting to be processed by someone—they've been there a while, it seems, being ignored, and in another day might no longer be good. The restaurant this weekend is so busy that no one on staff can possibly be spared to attend to them, so we decide to have at it. We set up a table behind the restaurant with one pot for hot water and another for finished peaches. Behind us the bird sanctuary twitters, and as we slide the skins off the soft, golden fruit, remove the pits, and cut up the flesh, fruit flies grow drunk on the aromatic, ripe debris. We are sitting and talking in the hot August sun, so obviously having a good time that one lodge guest—an old friend of the owner in town for the festival—comes out and asks if she can join us. It takes three hours to do all the peaches. Afterward we put them into Zip-Loc bags for freezing so Blake and Jen can make jam at their leisure. When we're through they feed us, and we can imagine no greater payment. Later, back home, our hands are still peach-golden—and they stay that way for days.

—DOLLY SPALDING

Stone-Fruit BBQ Sauce

This seriously easy and totally delicious spicy sauce is built around the most humble of ingredients: ketchup. Forgive. Use this sauce in the last 5 to 10 minutes of grilling meats; it's amazing with pork or chicken.

6 cups ketchup
¾ cup cider vinegar
3 tablespoons Worcestershire sauce
3 tablespoons soy sauce
2 cups brown sugar
¾ cup coarse ground mustard
2 tablespoons New Mexico chile powder
1 teaspoon cayenne
1 medium onion, diced small
4 cloves garlic, minced
2 teaspoons canola oil
1 lemon, in quarters, peel and all
3 cups chopped and pitted fresh sour cherries and/or apricots

Combine all ingredients in a medium saucepan over medium-low heat. Simmer for 1 hour, stirring often to keep sauce from sticking. Sauce will be rich, fragrant, and thick. Remove lemon quarters before serving.

75

Navajo-Style Peach Crisp

A Navajo family in Canyon De Chelly taught Blake this recipe. In Boulder we have many varieties of peaches, and this crisp is one of our favorite ways to use them. Eat it with fresh whipped cream, vanilla ice cream, or your bare hands.

FILLING

7 cups peeled and sliced fresh peaches
1 cup sugar
¼ cup white flour
2 tablespoons fresh lemon juice

TOPPING

1 cup white flour
⅔ cup yellow cornmeal
⅔ cup sugar
1 teaspoon salt
⅔ cup very cold butter cut into small pieces
    with a knife
½ cup toasted pine nuts

1. Preheat oven to 375 degrees. Butter an 8 x 10" baking dish.

2. **Filling:** In a medium bowl, combine peaches, sugar, flour, and lemon juice. Use your hands to really mix it well so no little flour lumps lurk anywhere. Spread the fruit mixture evenly in baking dish and set aside.

3. **Topping:** In a medium bowl, mix together flour, cornmeal, sugar, and salt. Using your fingers or the paddle attachment of a mixer, work butter pieces into the dry ingredients so the mixture looks like coarse crumbs. Mix in pine nuts.

4. Cover fruit evenly with topping. Set it on a baking sheet to catch any juices that spill over. Bake until fruit is bubbling and tender to a fork and topping is golden in color, about 45 minutes.

The Ice Cream Social

Ice cream is exquisite—what a pity it isn't illegal.

—VOLTAIRE

Each Independence Day, we throw our annual ice cream social, an event particularly close to our hearts. We hosted our first one the year we moved here, when we were still struggling to be accepted by the community. Things weren't easy for us—we had uprooted ourselves, moved to a tiny Mormon town where we knew no one, and then worked our tails off for weeks trying to fix up the restaurant, which had been closed for several months. We scrubbed and redecorated, caught and released the mice that had been living inside, danced around and sang and burned sage to clear the energy, strung Tibetan prayer flags outside. We shopped and ordered food and made menus and got excited. Then, when we finally felt ready to open, we hung a help-wanted sign, and not a single person applied. We felt disliked, isolated—had we made a tremendous mistake? Finally, Judi Davis, who ran the post office, took pity on us and encouraged her youngest daughter, Jennifer Davis, to apply for a job. Jennifer brought along her friend Krishell Heaton, and they became our first employees.

But people were still wary of newcomers and for the most part standoffish. No one was putting forth a lot of effort to welcome us. Jen had an idea: we could host an ice cream social. Timidly, we hung a sign at the post office inviting everyone to attend and bring their favorite topping. We had no idea if anyone would come, but we set up folding tables in front of the restaurant, uncovered the many tubs of ice cream we'd purchased, then waited to see what would happen. Almost the entire town arrived—car after car, family after family. People brought toppings and tried ours (chocolate chile, chocolate toasted piñon, butterscotch caramel, piñon brittle, white fondue fluff, cinnamon almond crusties), and the ice cream swiftly disappeared. Kids played on the lawn. We made friends. The mayor later told us he'd never seen so many of the townspeople together at one event before. It was, without a doubt, the beginning of our lives in Boulder.

A selection of our Fourth of July sundae toppings.

Cajeta Caramel Sauce with Piñons

Cajeta is a dessert sauce made from goat's milk. With a strong and distinct flavor, this thick sauce is the topping for an unusual sundae. Cajeta can also be made with a thinner consistency and drizzled over pound cake or apple-based desserts.

 4 cups white sugar
 1 cup water
 ⅓ cup unsalted butter
 ½ teaspoon salt
 1 cup goat's milk (can be purchased fresh or
   canned from most supermarkets)
 ¾ cup lightly toasted piñons (pine nuts)

1. In a heavy-bottomed, wide saucepan, bring sugar and water to a strong boil over high heat, stirring occasionally to dissolve sugar.

2. Once the mixture begins to boil, refrain from stirring and continue the steady boil to reduce liquid, bringing it to a light brown color (about 25 minutes). Pay close attention to color, thickness, and smell of the liquid. The color should be rich brown, the consistency honeylike, and the smell toasty but not burned.

3. Remove from heat and slowly stir in butter and salt. Immediately add goat's milk, stirring until completely blended. Add more or less milk to achieve the consistency you prefer.

4. Stir in toasted piñons. Taste and adjust the salt.

Hot Fudge Piñon Sauce

It's just so good! This sauce is soft, shiny, and chewy when spooned over ice cream. Makes enough sauce for about 8 drenched sundaes.

 ½ cup sugar
 ¼ cup unsweetened cocoa powder
 ¼ teaspoon salt
 ½ cup warm water
 1 cup heavy cream
 1 cup light corn syrup
 1 tablespoon white vinegar
 ⅓ cup semisweet chocolate chips
 2 ounces chopped unsweetened chocolate
 ¼ cup butter
 1 tablespoon vanilla extract
 2 cups pulverized piñons (pine nuts), plus 1
   cup well-toasted whole piñons for garnish

1. Sift sugar, cocoa powder, and salt into a medium saucepan. Add warm water and bring to a simmer over medium heat, stirring till smooth.

2. Add heavy cream, corn syrup, white vinegar, and chocolate chips. Boil on medium-high 10 to 15 minutes to reduce cream. Mixture will be thin and sticky. Remove from heat.

3. Stir in unsweetened chocolate, butter, vanilla extract, and pulverized piñons. Use sauce while it's still warm and garnish with additional piñons.

Cinnamon Sugared Almonds

Sprinkle these clusters on any dessert: ice cream, pudding, anything with whipped cream. Don't burn 'em, yo!

 2 cups sliced almonds
 ¾ cup white sugar
 1 tablespoon cinnamon
 ¼ cup water

Heat oven to 335 degrees. Stir all ingredients together in small mixing bowl. Spread on parchment-lined baking sheet and bake for 10 minutes. Stir nuts (they will be starting to look caramel-ish) and return to oven for 5 minutes. Let cool, and crumble candy apart with your fingers.

Old-Fashioned Butterscotch Pudding

This is the real deal, made the hard way with an authentic butterscotch beginning. It's wildly popular among the staff, with everyone sharing the scrapings from the pot.

> ½ cup heavy cream
> ¼ cup unsalted butter
> ¾ cup packed dark brown sugar
> ½ teaspoon salt
> 1½ cups whole milk
> 1 capful bourbon or Scotch whiskey
> 3 tablespoons water
> 3 tablespoons cornstarch

1. Measure out cream and put aside, within reach.

2. Melt butter over low heat in a heavy-bottomed saucepan. Stir in brown sugar and salt, and cook until completely melted and bubbling. It should look very smooth and start to have a slightly burned smell. This takes awhile, so be patient.

3. Gradually stir in cream, which will sputter and cause butterscotch to seize into candy. Don't worry! Keep stirring until butterscotch is dissolved. Add milk and whiskey and stir until blended. Remove from heat.

4. Measure out water and cornstarch, and mix the two together with your fingers until paste is smooth and free of lumps. Stir it into milk mixture, then cook, stirring constantly, over medium-high heat until it begins to thicken. Reduce heat to a low simmer and stir vigorously for 1 minute or more, until it thickly coats the back of the spoon.

5. Pour pudding into a bowl or individual cups, then press plastic wrap directly onto surface to prevent a skin from forming. It will store for a few days. If pudding separates or looks grainy, just give it a quick whirl in the food processor, and it will be restored to glossy. We serve it topped with freshly whipped cream and a shard of piñon chile brittle.

Piñon Chile Brittle

We top our butterscotch pudding with this candy, but it's equally delicious by itself or crushed as an ice cream topping. It also stores well and makes a terrific gift. Candy making is a skill that requires patience and practice, so be kind to yourself.

> ¾ cup piñons (pine nuts)
> ½ teaspoon guajillo chile powder
> ½ teaspoon pasilla negro chile powder
> ½ teaspoon cloves
> ½ teaspoon salt
> 1½ cups sugar

1. Line a baking sheet with parchment paper and spray it with a nonstick vegetable oil.

2. In a small cast-iron or nonstick skillet, toast piñons by stirring them over low heat until they're a light golden brown. Set aside.

3. Combine chile, cloves, salt, and sugar in a larger nonstick skillet. Over medium heat, melt sugar, stirring constantly until it's a smooth caramel with a rich dark brown color. There's a very fine line between caramel and burned sugar, so pay attention. When the sugar is entirely melted, quickly stir in the piñons.

4. Immediately pour molten sugar onto lined baking sheet, tipping the sheet if necessary to achieve an evenly distributed sheet of candy.

5. Let it cool until hard and solid, then break into pieces to serve. This candy is best stored in a dry place at room temperature.

An American in Boulder

Wheresoever you go, go with all your heart.

—CONFUCIUS

It's six-thirty in the morning, still dark, and I'm tiptoeing across my older sister's living room, avoiding the places that creak. I'm sneaking out of her house, off to work the breakfast shift at the restaurant. I inch open the front door and am nearly outside when I hear her faint, sleepy voice call out.

"Bye, honey," she says, her voice a blend of apology and gratitude. It's the same thing each time I work this shift—no matter how quiet I am, she can't sleep through my exit. And by this point it's become almost a challenge to me, though I realize it's probably hopeless. Blake knows I'm the anti-morning person, that I have been my entire life. She knows that until I moved to Boulder from Korea two months ago to work at the restaurant, I rarely made it out of bed before noon. Furthermore, she recognizes herself as the force behind this upheaval in my routine, and she feels sorry about it.

I call out good-bye, my voice a blend of faked perkiness and sincere absolution. It's OK, I attempt to communicate—you stay where you are. You're tired. You work too much. Sleep.

Then I'm out the door, into my car. The road breathes out before me in total silence, and my headlights illuminate the tiny, beautiful world of lower Boulder. To my right, sandstone buttes like enormous caramel-cream cakes for giants, to my left, Annie's fruit orchard where Blake and I occasionally pick apples to eat on our walks.

In front of my tired, cobwebbed eyes, a doe and two fawns spring gracefully across the road. I tap my brakes gently, yawn, watch as they run off through the horse-filled pasture. If it weren't for wildlife all over the road, I think to myself, I could close my eyes and the car would probably autopilot itself to work.

Though I've been here only a few months, this drive, the easy one-mile cruise between Blake's cottage and the restaurant, has become as familiar to me as any road I've ever known. While I'm at it, I could easily say the same about the town of Boulder.

I remember my first dinner shift at the restaurant—the clientele that evening a smattering of tourists and locals. By the end of the night, I'd received a dinner invitation from a local couple, an offer of lodging from a girl living in the next town over, a handful of tourists' business cards, and the phone number of a customer's single son. After residing most of my adult life in big cities where anonymity was practically an ordinance, this sudden outpouring of

love and attention was somewhat confusing. Was it for real? Would it be this way every night?

It was for real, I would discover, and yes, it would be this way nearly every day and night. And what's more, I would even sort of get used to it.

Over the following months I learned the local wave, the one executed from your automobile as a greeting to any oncoming vehicle (the key to a perfect Boulder wave, I'd been coached, was to look casual, which meant never actually lifting your hand from the steering wheel). I learned the names of Boulder's children, its dogs, horses, even its pet pigs. I learned to stop locking my car and to leave the key in the ignition, because that way you never had to look for it; you always knew where it was. And gradually, I learned to accept inclusion into a community where anonymity was not only out of the ordinary, it was virtually unattainable.

Pulling into the driveway of the restaurant, I spot the remnants of last night's Fourth of July festivities. Flags poke patriotically out of the fence on the grounds in front of the restaurant, and the stage where the town talent show was held is still standing. (All Blake's stereo equipment remains there as well, having spent a peaceful, unmolested night on the lawn.)

Every year the restaurant hosts an ice cream social, but this year Blake and Jen decided to put on a talent show as well. Concerned that the number of participants might be skimpy, they urged all their employees to compete. (As it turned out, they needn't have worried—just about the whole town came out.) I chose to play the guitar. I'd had my misgivings (a lifetime of stage fright will do that to a person), but in the end I agreed. After all, I reasoned, this was Boulder, Utah, population 180: surely a forgiving venue. I hadn't lived here long enough for most people to know me, and the few who recognized me would hardly remember the next day if I made a few mistakes. I practiced my guitar for about an hour and got up on stage. Halfway through my piece, I forgot what I was playing, froze, and stopped.

"I'm sorry," I said and, mumbling something incoherent about stage fright, ran offstage.

Oh well, I thought. That was embarrassing.

The restaurant is still dark when I arrive, and completely quiet. I flip on the lights and start the coffee. After a few

older woman with gray hair. She waves and smiles at me and looks vaguely familiar. A local, I assume, or a lodge guest I've served a few times. When I bring her coffee, she puts her hand gently on my wrist.

"Honey," she says, "you sounded so good last night. I just have to tell you, I think you're awfully brave getting up there when you have stage fright." I mumble an embarrassed "thank you" and attempt to leave. Apparently unaware of my desperation to escape, however, she goes on a bit, so that when the next customers arrive I practically sprint to their table.

Except they have a similar opening line.

"You should've kept playing last night!" they exclaim. "It was wonderful! How did you learn to play the classical guitar? How long have you been playing?"

At this point I decide to spend my morning hiding in the kitchen. I will come out only when absolutely necessary.

By the time my shift ends at two, a total of seven tables have delivered addresses on my botched performance, offering up everything from encouragement to commiseration to tips on combating performance anxiety. I'm relieved to be off work. I plan to disappear for the rest of the day, but before that happens I need to stop by the post office. As I get out of my car and head to the mailbox to drop off a letter, a woman I've never seen before in my life suddenly halts her pickup truck in the middle of the road, gets out, and hurries around the front of the truck.

"I have to tell you," she calls out to me. She plays the organ, it seems, in the church here. And she has these people trained. These Boulder ears are used to hearing mistakes. They would've never known. She is of the opinion that I should have kept playing.

Finally, I'm back in my car. I have my mail and am en route back to Blake's, down the same familiar road. As I round the corner where this morning I saw the deer, I pass a neighbor from up the road. We both do the steering wheel wave, but then he slows down, stops, rolls down his window, and tells me what he thinks.

As we say good-bye and I drive on, I realize I'm smiling. Then I realize I'm home.

minutes, Jennifer Davis arrives to do the cooking. Little Jenny D, as we call her, was Blake and Jen's first employee, and at the restaurant is unanimously adored. I let her choose the opening tunes (she picks a top-forty mix, cranking songs by boy bands and fast-forwarding through any containing adult lyrics), and she lets me eat the first, trial, blue-corn pancake of the day. It's our usual routine.

At seven o'clock sharp, my first customer arrives. She's an

— LAVINIA SPALDING

It's a Dog's Life

The dog wags his tail not for you, but for your bread.

—PORTUGUESE PROVERB

When you own a restaurant and dogs as well, your dogs eventually become, well, restaurant dogs. This means they hang out in the back and occasionally nudge open the screen door when you're not watching and trot happily through the dining room, sniffing the floor and greeting customers, who are almost invariably as delighted by the arrival of your dogs as your dogs are to be at their tables. Your dogs gradually acquire a taste for organic vegetables and come to know precisely which buckets hold compost and what glorious bounty lies within. (We call the compost buckets "the doggie buffet.") Over the years they become as much a part of the restaurant as the flowers on the table, the music on the stereo, the guests, and the employees.

Our returning customers ask after our dogs with such regularity that we feel we would be remiss not talking about them just a little.

Tashi

Blake's dog Tashi was a gift from the Bowns, ranchers from Gunnison who supply our organic lamb and also happen to raise hunting dogs. After Blake's old dog Echo died, she resisted getting a new puppy, until one night she dreamt her tiny cat was a dog, barking at an intruder. When she arrived at the grill that day, Lynn Bown was waiting for her. Lynn's lab had given birth to six puppies that morning—would Blake like a chocolate lab puppy? she asked. Blake had always wanted a chocolate lab. Lynn usually sold her dogs, but this time she didn't.

"Oh my heck, I couldn't have charged Blake," Lynn says. "I didn't feel right about charging her. She needed a companion—and it must have been meant to be because the timing was perfect."

Tashi, whose full name is Tashi Deleg ("auspicious good fortune" in Tibetan), is effusive, gentle, and unfailingly patient (she lives with four cats; she doesn't really have a choice). When she sees a child, she rolls on her back and plays peekaboo, crossing her paws over her eyes so the children won't be afraid. She loves broccoli. But what really distinguishes Tashi from other dogs is that she's quite possibly the only canine in America to have been invited to dine with a Tibetan lama. The situation sprang from Tashi's innate belief that she's a human being, an idea

that manifests in various ways but mostly at the dinner table, when she climbs up into a chair like a child and sits with perfect posture throughout dinner, never trying to snack off anyone's plate, simply enjoying being present as one of the adults. One year when the monks of the Drepung Loseling Monastery were in town, Tashi chose the best seat in the house—beside the geshe, the honored and esteemed lama, head of the monks. After this, the geshe began saving Tashi a spot next to him.

Lily

Lily is Jen's dog, yes, but over the years Jen has been forced to confront the fact that while Lily lives with her and wears a tag bearing her name as owner, she must share custody. Lily belongs not exclusively to Jen, not even to Jen and one or two other people. Lily belongs to the world.

"People return to Boulder to see her," Jen says. "Not me. Her. One lady hassled me about it, insisting I wasn't her owner. 'No, the girl was on a bike,' she said. Cooing at Lily, trying to convince me I wasn't the one she'd met."

Lily loves vegetables and taught her little sister Tashi how to eat them. She does not love fireworks, ponchos, sombreros, or frame backpacks. She's nice to cats. Lily loves most people but is hopelessly devoted to BJ. She's an incredible hiking partner and is very communicative. She rarely barks except when fighting sticks, harassing horses, protecting someone she loves, or feeling offended by dog riffraff. But she talks a lot, in a voice similar to the Hamburglar. And she never bites. She was raised using the methods of the Monks of New Skete (the best puppy training manual in existence) and could sit on command at ten weeks. While she has never been formally tested, we have no reason to doubt she's a genius.

(Sure-footed and well balanced, Lily is the dog of the future! Order your Lily2000 today!)

Lily (top) and Tashi (bottom) make our lives complete.

Autumn

Autumn

If you want your dreams to come true, don't sleep.

—YIDDISH PROVERB

The fall season for us is a bit like an amusement park ride. In September the weather begins to cool, a second wave of wildflowers blooms, and the aspens on the mountain turn a fiery gold. Everything glimmers and sparkles magically, and we fall easily under the spell, blinded by flashes of yellow leaves against red sandstone. Apparently forgetting what this particular ride feels like, we gamely buy our tickets and climb aboard. And it's just lovely at first. Just lovely, really. On afternoon strolls with our dogs we collect leaves and heart-shaped stones. In the evenings we drink wine on the deck with our artist and photographer friends who visit from out of town. We meet with brides and their anxious mothers to plan menus for our fall weddings. Just lovely, really. And then, BAM! Someone flicks a switch and we're jerked forward, whipped around fiercely, hung upside down and spun. Every night the dining room is packed; we're throwing wedding receptions each weekend for the brides and their mothers (anxious before but now completely possessed); we've eighty-sixed everything on the menu except chicken and tap water, and half our staff has abandoned us to go on missions or return to school. We're so short-handed that every night Blake chooses one customer she likes and attempts to hypnotize him or her into staying in Boulder to work for us. We're alarmed by how long we've been in this position—upside down and spinning—but there's no getting off. All we can do is hold tight, scream, and try not to get sick.

Fall, if further clarification is required, is our busiest season—and resistance? Futile. The only course of action during these months is to surrender to the chaos—try, in fact, to *love* the chaos. It's pandemonium from garden to dining room to kitchen, and just as in spring (and lately summer, too), accruing more than six hours of sleep is a comic notion. Every guidebook hails autumn as the time to visit Utah, and these instructions are dutifully obeyed by tourists from all over the Southwest. And the Northwest. As well as the rest of the country. Not to mention Europe. Thanks in large part to our providential location on Highway 12—a magnificent scenic byway designated as a Great American Highway (one of only eight in the United States) and named one of the country's ten most scenic drives by *Car and Driver* magazine—we see our fair share of those travelers. Nature writers and journalists, family vacationers and honeymooners, backpackers and tour groups. A regular presence in fall are bands of motorcyclists roaring up to the grill, filling the front parking spots with a domino-like row of Harleys and infusing the dining room with the thud of boots and the smell of leather. And the other bikers, groups of cyclists pedaling hundreds of miles a day, famished to the point of almost fainting on our front steps. Fall demands sixteen-hour workdays from us. At one point we leave the restaurant and drive four hours round-trip to Richfield, the sole reason to buy a new, vitally needed microwave. We blearily purchase the microwave and promptly forget all about it—leaving it behind. Back in Boulder, it takes us two days to notice the oversight, more than a week for Jen to call the store, and two weeks before she has time to drive back to Richfield to pick it up.

Autumn is also the time when, as Blake says, "that hole in the ground where we put money starts producing for us." That hole, our garden, represents vision, principles, commitment to environmental responsibility, plotting, determination, and extremely hard work. It does not, unfortunately, represent a return on investment. The fact is we'd save heaps of money if we purchased all our vegetables en masse from Somewhere Far Away. In Somewhere Far Away, everything is perpetually in season. *Everything.* We can have pink strawberries in November and orange pumpkins in May from Somewhere Far Away. And while Somewhere Far Away is unarguably a beguiling, mysterious place, we regretfully decline—insofar as possible—the opportunity to procure food from Somewhere Far Away. It costs us roughly the same amount of money to pull one ripe tomato from our garden as it does to order ten from Somewhere Far Away. The fact that we continue to pull that one tomato and fight the temptation to order the other ten might suggest an impressive lack of business sense. Not to us. On the contrary, we believe it to be a principal explanation for why Helles still breathes today: food not grown in a hothouse and shipped thousands of miles to reach the dinner plate is spared the discomfort of culture shock; it isn't road-weary or jet-lagged. It's fresh and real and more flavorsome. We're especially careful not to grow anything we can't utilize; we're experimental but not frivolous, and more than anything, we're locally inspired. What we plant is appropriate, suited to alkaline soil, sustainable, and easily grown in high desert.

"What's neat about the restaurant is that it gets people thinking about where their food comes from," says Ana Rendón, one of our

Opposite: Cast-iron Dutch ovens hold a place of honor in Mormon frontier cooking, heritage, and culture. We use them at the grill regularly because after years as river cooks, we just can't get 'em out of our systems. Here Ellayna and Blake deliver a roasted apple and pear cobbler. Top right: Kayenta Ryan stands in the doorway of the family's home, a custom-made yurt. Bottom right: Roasted red bell peppers from the restaurant's organic garden.

gardeners. "They look out the window and see that they're eating vegetables and herbs from the garden just outside. Hopefully it's inspiring people to be more curious and to continue exploring the possibilities of growing their own food."

So, happily, the onset of fall invites, in addition to more customers, a bounty of produce. In spring and summer our gardeners are forced to be judicious harvesters, observing a delicate balance—picking enough to feed the day's customers but not overpicking, lest there isn't enough for tomorrow. In fall we're spared that worry. Aware that frost could kill the entire garden in a single night, we harvest like crazy—tomatoes, carrots, Swiss chard, cabbage, pumpkins, and several varieties of hard squashes. (We're also among the last in Boulder to attempt growing corn—the raccoons here wreak havoc on corn crops, and locals once went to enormous lengths to repel them, even trying, with reportedly fair results, leaving television sets turned on in gardens.) In the late months, we discuss the weather every day to determine the necessity of covering the gardens. Usually we do so, with old sheets and tablecloths, and make no mistake: it is a fantastic pain in the neck. The garden, for us, represents a potent metaphor for the commitment we keep to upholding our value system. It can often be difficult to maintain, and the rewards are seldom instant or even very apparent. But then we take the first bite of the first tomato and in a nanosecond remember why it all matters so much.

We strive constantly to make the food we serve an honest reflection of our location, not only geographically but culturally and historically. Gardening, picking, and canning are deep community traditions in Boulder—not merely as hobby but rather as necessity. The community is comprised largely of subsistence farmers with the resources to survive a year of privation. They keep fifty-five gallons of grain in their basements, and their recipe for survival is stretching, stocking, and preserving. In efforts to observe and incorporate local traditions and beliefs, we've found many of them compatible to our own—the LDS code of no poisons, for instance, includes pesticides and additives, and as a result many church members grow organically. Furthermore, we depend on all manner of rural wisdom and invaluable gardening advice dispensed from locals. No one in town puts a thing in the ground until Veda Behunin, a longtime local who's still gardening at ninety, begins planting—which she won't do until the snow has melted in a certain notch on the mountains. Veda watches the notch from her house in town, and everyone in town watches her.

We source locally to the best of our ability. On various levels this is gratifying—it endorses local commerce, and the produce tastes wonderful—but it's also unpredictable and a very in-the-

Top left: Well, we try. Bottom left: Regular customer Holly Hopper and her son Remmy at breakfast. Right: Jen presents a Thanksgiving side dish.

moment method of running a restaurant. Yes, local honey tastes better. It also runs out. Lambs are born only in late spring because of the winters here. And if a local crop freezes and dies, we won't get our expected produce. One solution is to scamper to the phone, call SYSCO, frantically order what we need from Somewhere Far Away, and wait anxiously for its arrival in a week. Sometimes there's no way around doing that, but more often we choose solution number two—change the menu and use something we do have. It works for us. We'll never be the restaurant that offers the same cuisine every time a customer comes—we couldn't be if we tried, nor would we want to be. Of course, customers grow attached to certain menu items, crying, "Oh, I'm so disappointed you don't have the chocolate bread pudding!" But, you know, we've eaten in corporate restaurants where the menu items never change. And sure, the food always tastes good, but do we remember our meals? Not even hardly.

Our menu reflects the change of season as well. Cold weather warrants heartier food, so our recipes become a bit more involved and substantial. The rest of the year we serve our garden vegetables fresh and unadorned, but in the fall we love to make slow-roasted thyme carrots, warm red cabbage salad with hazelnuts, root vegetable gratin, pureed sweet potatoes with Utah goat cheese, butternut squash soup with sizzled sage, and maple-glazed squash rings. For dessert, we might serve poached pears in red wine with juniper berries and cinnamon. And for breakfast, appropriately autumnal dishes such as dreamy, creamy, hot and steamy oatmeal served with caramelized apple compote, and The Elvis, a thick slice of our homemade oatmeal-molasses bread stuffed with almond butter and bacon, French-toasted in a thick bath of eggs, sugar, and cream, and topped with hot buttered maple sauce. This is the one that inspires parents to send their children away so they won't witness Mom and Dad licking their plates.

October is busy, but we try to take the time to host a Halloween party. The occasion is a little different in Boulder from the rest of the world; it's a genuinely old-fashioned affair here, with many of the children in town making their own costumes. We prepare popcorn balls and whoopie pies at the grill to give away, and Jen hauls out her karaoke machine so we can fight the kids for the microphone.

Starting in November, things slow down considerably while we prepare for our end-of-season hurrah, Thanksgiving weekend. Our Thanksgiving reservations begin rolling in a year in advance. We offer two dinner seatings and serve everyone family-style, with two kinds of free-range turkey—honey chile-roasted and sage-rubbed—and ten or twelve accompanying dishes, which might include chestnut pumpkin soup, spinach salad with a warm pear vinaigrette, chicken liver pâté with currants and calvados, dried cherry and cranberry compote, red chile gravy, and for dessert, chocolate-chile pecan pie, pumpkin

cheesecake, and Annie's Orchard roasted apple-pear cobbler.

Then it's over. We've somehow made it through to winter and finally have the doctor's permission to give Helles a sedative as we close the restaurant for three whole months.

We stumble off the amusement park ride, tired, ragged, dizzy, lightheaded, and wobbly. Our stomachs are turned inside out and our hair sticks up in odd places, and at last we sit, and swear we'll never do that again.

Manna from Heaven

A freakishly food-obsessed nine-year-old customer named this dish. It was created as a way to use our leftover cornbread muffins and easily became a breakfast favorite. Do not skip the manna sauce, a hot buttered maple delight that you'll want to drink for breakfast. Nor is the heavy cream in the recipe to be substituted, as it allows the manna to take the heat without burning.

> ¾ cup heavy cream
> 3 eggs
> 1 teaspoon vanilla extract
> ⅛ teaspoon salt
> ½ cup powdered sugar
> 1 tablespoon butter
> 2 cups crumbled leftover cornbread

1. Preheat oven to broil. Whisk together cream, eggs, vanilla extract, salt, and sugar in a small mixing bowl.

2. Heat a nonstick 6" oven-proof skillet on the stovetop on medium-high, melting 1 tablespoon butter.

3. Crumble cornbread into egg mixture, keeping pieces a little chunky. With a slotted spoon, transfer cornbread and most of the liquid to hot skillet.

4. As the edges of the cake begin to firm, push a third of it from the edge in toward the middle using a rubber spatula, letting the wet run underneath and filling the space left behind, as you would an omelette. Repeat for each third, then remove from heat.

5. Place skillet in oven for just 2 to 3 minutes, until the top of the manna cake is firm, puffed, and golden. Invert or slide onto serving plate. Douse with manna maple sauce and share it if you can bear it.

Manna Maple Sauce

Serve this warm over our signature cornbread French toast, Manna from Heaven.

> 1 cup maple syrup
> ⅓ cup sugar
> 6 tablespoons butter in 1" pieces
> 2 tablespoons water
> ⅛ teaspoon salt
> 1 egg

1. In small, heavy saucepan combine maple syrup and sugar over medium heat. Bring to a gentle boil, stirring with a wooden spoon 8 to 10 minutes until the last drop that falls from the spoon resembles a thread. The bubbling mixture will be foamy.

2. Remove from heat and add butter, water, and salt, stirring till the butter has melted. Mixture will react and sputter initially.

3. In a small bowl whisk the egg. Slowly whisk the hot maple mixture into egg, then return everything to saucepan. Bring sauce to an easy boil over medium heat, about 3 minutes, to thicken. If you find you have scrambled-egg pieces in your sauce, please strain them out.

The Ryan Family

*To be able under all circumstances to practice five things constitutes perfect virtue;
these five things are gravity, generosity of soul, sincerity, earnestness and kindness.*

—CONFUCIUS

Mike and Carrie Ryan and their daughters Kayenta and Willow live almost exactly halfway between our two homes, which puts them approximately a quarter-mile from both of us. What a visitor first sees is a large, impressive, two-story, board-on-board structure, like a barn or house. It's neither, though; it's what they call their "closet." Where they live is actually behind that, in a yurt sixteen feet in diameter—roughly one-fourth the size of the closet.

Mike and Carrie are Boulder Outdoor Survival School (BOSS) instructors and live, in just about every way, incredibly close to the earth. They've been in Boulder off and on for twenty years and have proven to be an invaluable resource for us on everything from frontier-style cooking and preserving to gardening.

The Ryans are subsistence farmers; they buy their grains and beans but grow or forage almost everything else. Nearly all the vegetables they eat come from their garden, or gardens rather, since Kayenta and Willow have tended their own since they were three or four years old. Each year the girls design their plots and decide what to grow, then do all the planting and maintenance themselves. Last year Willow, age six, planted peppers, cherry tomatoes, cucumbers for pickling, and peas. Kayenta, at nine, went for scarlet runner beans, lemon cucumbers, and a mass of flowers.

Because they actually live on the food they grow, the Ryans' garden is extensive, and occasionally there's excess produce. What Carrie can't use she often brings to the grill.

"I don't want to waste anything valuable. I've taken up garbage bags of salad from my garden, and Blake and Jen always find something to trade for it. They value clean food, unadulterated by chemicals, something many people don't understand. To have a restaurant that serves clean food is amazing."

Near the front door of the Ryans' "closet," cardboard boxes filled with garlic or cabbage cover the floor, and the shelves to the left are lined with jars: canned sauerkraut, green beans, and veggie

juice, not to mention medicinal salves made by Mike and Carrie from plants soaked in olive oil, then strained and infused with beeswax, grapefruit-seed extract, chaparral, or vitamin E. Across from the shelves sits a contraption that resembles an abandoned exercise bike but is in fact an ingenious bicycle-powered mill used to grind grain for cereals and baking. The second floor of the closet holds winnowing baskets, corrugated pots, linens, clothes, books, and camping gear. Aboriginal-style objects abound, including shoes made from agave. In the corner is a box of bones from which they'll craft buttons, hair pins, fishhooks, and knives. And on a shelf above the desk where the girls do arts and crafts and where Carrie does her sewing, gigantic rolls of moose, elk, and deer rawhide. It's the biggest, weirdest, most organized closet anyone's ever seen.

Carrie is Boulder's Cub Scout leader, and Mike is the town Boy Scout leader. Before working for BOSS, they used to work with troubled teens. "Now we're working on prevention," Carrie says, motioning to the girls. But it's hard to imagine these kids ever being troubled. Kayenta and Willow are the quintessential prairie girls, gentle and almost frighteningly smart. They wear braids to their waists and dresses sewn by Carrie, attend church, study sign language, and sometimes leave bouquets of wildflowers with crayoned notes for Blake on her coffee table when she's not home. You can't see these girls growing up anywhere else. Boulder is made for the Ryans.

"Boulder's different in that you don't have to wear certain clothes, makeup, or nylons, even to church," Carrie says. "You can be as weird as you want. You're accepted even if you're different—because everyone's different here. It's the most eclectic community you can think of. It's not a typical southern Utah community."

Even so, it isn't always easy for newcomers. "Blake jumped right into the fire. I don't think she knew what she was getting into. But she and Jen have tried to create a peaceful, safe community and bring everyone together. The activities they've done really include the town. The talent show, for example—it was a fluke how it happened, but it's been a great thing. A lot of people came, and it was safe. And Blake and Jen try to go to all the town functions. And I think it's good for members of the community to work at the grill, because it's a social thing.

Willow Ryan, six, tends her garden. Each year she and Kayenta design, plant, and maintain their own plots.

Willow plays with Tashi on the Ryan family property.

They've tried so hard to engage all the townspeople in some way."

The Ryans' yurt is small, cozy, and custom-made. There's a kitchen, dining room, and living room, and they've added a loft (where Kayenta and Willow sleep) and windows. They use an RV battery to run two lights and a boom box. Otherwise, there's no electricity, no running water, no telephone, and no bathroom. The oven is a tin box set on their woodstove. It's small inside the Ryan home, but not cramped. It's the kind of place where you want to relax, learn, make something with your hands, enjoy the company.

One winter Blake was planning to go away to do a two-week Buddhist retreat, but at the time Tashi was only seven months old, and she knew she couldn't leave her new puppy with a friend for that long. She decided to try a solitary home retreat, which meant purchasing all the food she'd need in advance and letting everyone know she wouldn't be answering her phone or door. She hung a "silent retreat" sign on her gate and got ready to disappear for ten days. A few days into the retreat, she let Tashi out in the morning and saw that a basket of food had been left on her front step by Carrie. Inside was breakfast: acorn flour pancakes and elderberry syrup.

"That's something that happened to me," Carrie explained,

"when we first came here. We didn't have anything, but I knew we weren't going to starve. A neighbor brought canned peaches, others offered apples, squash, melons. That's something that ought to be passed on."

Behind the yurt is the family shower, which Carrie describes as "basically a basket." Next to that stands the framework of a wickiup, arched poles waiting to be filled in and covered with duff. "That'll be our guest room," Carrie says, smiling. Fruit trees are scattered around—apples, peaches, nectarines, pears, cherries, and a whole slew of berries: blackberries, strawberries, elderberries, goose-berries, and Nanking cherries. There's a massive pile of wood they've chopped themselves and a hide wringer. And strung up on the back side of the closet, two enormous bison hides, seven feet high by eight feet across. One will be made into a container and a blanket. The other's fate is not yet decided.

"In Boulder," Carrie says, "people still know how to make meat from start to finish. Most people still have gardens. Everyone's just really self-sufficient. Even if the world got really bad, really crazy, this place would pull together in a big way. It has the most potential for people to live cooperatively."

Dreamy Creamed Swiss Chard

In high-altitude gardens, Swiss chard is a natural. You can plant it early, it will survive frosts, and it's pest tolerant, abundant, and beautiful to look at. Every year we end up planting more rows of chard to meet the demand for this popular autumn side dish.

1½ tablespoons butter
1 cup diced onion
1 teaspoon minced garlic
1 pound fresh Swiss chard, cleaned and
    chopped into thin ribbons (we use the
    tender part of the stems as well)
1½ cups heavy cream
½ cup grated Parmesan
1 cup dried or fresh biscuit crumbs (bread
    crumbs are a fine substitute)
1½ tablespoons fresh tarragon (dried will
    work, but reduce amount to 1 teaspoon)
1½ teaspoons salt
1 teaspoon coarse ground pepper

1. Melt butter in a large, heavy-bottomed saucepan. Sauté onion in butter until it's soft and starting to turn golden.

2. Add garlic and cook gently for a few minutes. Add the chopped Swiss chard and give it all a good stir. Pour in cream and let simmer for five minutes or so, then add grated cheese, biscuit crumbs, tarragon, salt, and pepper. Gently stir to combine everything. The thickness of the mixture can be adjusted by adding a little extra milk or cream.

3. Cook for about 10 minutes, occasionally stirring gently until the chard is tender and the mixture has a pleasing, thick consistency. Adjust salt and pepper to taste.

Warm Red Cabbage Salad with Goat Cheese

This salad is served in the fall as an appetizer plate or as an accompaniment to pork. The color is beautiful, and the flavors dance in your mouth.

¼ cup canola oil
1 medium-sized head of red cabbage, sliced into thin shreds
⅔ cup chopped and lightly toasted hazelnuts or piñons (pine nuts)
⅓ cup high-quality balsamic vinegar
1 tablespoon sugar
½ teaspoon sea salt
4 ounces fresh goat cheese (chèvre)

1. In a medium-sized sauté pan, gently heat oil. Add cabbage and ½ cup of the nuts. Sauté until cabbage is wilted, stirring frequently.

2. Add balsamic vinegar, sugar, and salt and cook for another minute, stirring well to coat the cabbage mixture. Taste to make certain cabbage is tender enough and to adjust the seasonings. Add more salt or vinegar if it needs brightening.

3. Transfer a portion of the cabbage to a salad plate and crumble an ounce of goat cheese over each salad. Sprinkle with a teaspoon of additional chopped nuts. Serve warm.

Toasted Piñon Dressing

A robust dressing that graces our menu in the early spring and fall, it's best served on hardier greens like spinach. When they are locally available, we top the salad with pomegranate seeds.

⅓ cup onion, chopped and sautéed
¾ cup cider vinegar
1 tablespoon Dijon mustard
⅓ cup honey
1 tablespoon salt
1½ cups canola oil
1½ cups toasted piñons (pine nuts)

1. In a blender, mix onion, vinegar, Dijon mustard, honey, and salt.

2. With blender running, drizzle oil over mixture. When emulsified, add the toasted piñons and blend till smooth, adding just a few teaspoons of water if the mixture is too thick.

Hopi Lamb Stuffed Peppers

This recipe is fashioned after a traditional Pueblo Indian dish, using simple ingredients to make a memorable dinner.

8 red bell peppers, one-quarter of sides carved off to create pepper boats, green stems intact
1 pound ground lamb
½ onion, finely chopped
2 tomatoes, roughly chopped
3 cloves garlic
2 teaspoons thyme
1 teaspoon red pepper flakes
½ teaspoon cayenne (optional)
2 tablespoons salt
1 tablespoon pepper
2 cups cooked posole corn (may substitute 28-ounce can whole white hominy, drained)
½ cup warmed honey
1 cup toasted piñons (pine nuts)
1 egg, slightly beaten
1 cup pepper jack cheese, cut into 1" cubes

1. Remove all seeds and membranes from peppers. Steam red peppers to soften, 7 to 10 minutes over boiling water. Set aside.

2. Sauté ground lamb and onion in large skillet over medium heat until onion softens and meat is browned. Add tomato, garlic, spices, salt, and pepper and cook 1 more minute. Transfer to a large mixing bowl.

3. Add drained posole corn, honey, and piñons to the bowl and stir well. Adjust seasonings to taste. Toss in beaten egg and cheese cubes.

4. Spoon filling into pepper boats, heaping slightly. Place in a greased 9 x 11" baking dish, nestling the peppers to fit snugly. Bake in preheated 350-degree oven for 25 to 35 minutes until peppers are soft, filling is hot, and tops are starting to crisp.

Chicken Liver Pâté with Currants

This recipe is beloved even by determined liver haters. It's a standard at weddings, parties, and celebrations and is featured on our menu in the fall. It's best made a day ahead so the flavors have a chance to mingle and get to know one another. We serve it with little breads or toasts.

12 peppercorns
5 cups water
2 teaspoons salt
1 pound organic or free-range chicken livers
½ teaspoon cayenne
½ pound (2 sticks) softened butter
2½ teaspoons dry mustard
½ teaspoon ground cloves
½ teaspoon grated nutmeg
1 minced garlic clove
¼ cup cognac or calvados
¾ cup currants

1. In a saucepan, bring water, peppercorns, and salt to a boil. Reduce heat and add livers. Simmer gently for approximately 10 to 12 minutes. The livers should be cooked through but still a bit pink inside.

2. Drain livers, removing peppercorns and any excess sludge.

3. Place livers into a food processor with the rest of the ingredients (except currants) and process the pâté for as long as it takes to become really smooth.

4. Stir in currants by hand.

5. Dish the pâté into a pretty 3- to 4-cup crock or a few smaller bowls and smooth out the top with a rubber spatula or butter knife. Refrigerate overnight or at least 5 hours before serving. Let the pâté stand at room temperature for 30 minutes before serving.

Roasted Poblano Cream Pasta Sauce

This heavy-duty cream sauce is our most popular. It's particularly divine topped with strips of grilled organic chicken and crumbles of snappy Utah goat cheese. Serve over fettuccine or linguine and prepare to fall out of your chair.

We put the cooled pasta into a few tablespoons of the sauce, using a splash of cream to thin it out a bit.

1 yellow onion, roughly chopped
1 tablespoon salt
½ cup white wine or broth
6 roasted red peppers or roasted poblano chiles, peeled and seeded
2 garlic cloves, peeled
4 cups heavy cream
½ tablespoon pepper

1. In a wide shallow skillet, cook onion and 1 tablespoon salt on medium-low heat for 10 minutes, shaking pan occasionally. When onion softens and there are brown bits stuck to pan, pour in wine to loosen bits.

2. Add roasted red peppers or green chile and garlic cloves and cook for 10 minutes.

3. Add heavy cream and pepper. Bring to a slow, lazy simmer with small bubbles around the outer edge of pan. Cook for 40 minutes, reducing volume by one-third.

4. Blend in food processor or with a hand-held immersion blender until the mixture is beautifully smooth.

The Question of Fish

Every now and then customers look at our menu and ask where the seafood is. We don't tell them we think they're being impolite. Instead, we gently remind them they're dining in the high desert, and if someone tries to serve them seafood out here, it's (excuse the pun, but we cannot seem to help ourselves) a bit fishy.

We serve only one fish, because it's the only one relevant to our location: a red-fleshed trout available to us as a fresh and a smoked fillet. Due to USDA regulations, we're not allowed to serve wild-caught freshwater fish. Our trout is farm-raised in Loa, about fifty miles away, so it coincides with our place-based philosophy—also, it's just plain delicious.

Cowboy Skillet Trout

Perhaps you've been fishing all weekend and want to wow the room with an all-new trout flavor sensation. This is your moment.

1. Fillet 2 fresh trout.

2. In a shallow baking dish, marinate the fillets over-night (refrigerated) in the molasses mixture (recipe follows).

3. Heat ½" canola oil in a 12" cast-iron skillet until almost smoking.

4. Remove fish from marinade and dredge flesh side in cornmeal-pecan breading (recipe follows).

5. Fry 2 fillets at a time, skin side down and breading side up, for 4 to 5 minutes. Flip each fillet and fry a minute or 2 more, until edges are crispy and bubbles form on the skin side of the fish. Remove from oil with a slotted spatula and flip onto paper towels to drain, skin side now down. Repeat with the last 2 fillets.

Molasses Marinade

½ cup honey
½ cup molasses
1 tablespoon granulated garlic
¼ cup Dijon mustard

Measure ingredients into a 2-cup Pyrex measuring cup and microwave 30 seconds to make mixture easy to stir. Pour over fish fillets. Flip to coat.

Cornmeal–Pecan Trout Breading

1 cup toasted pecan pieces
1 cup breadcrumbs
½ cup cornmeal
½ teaspoon salt
1 teaspoon pepper
½ teaspoon granulated garlic
2 teaspoons New Mexican chile powder

Combine all ingredients in food processor fitted with blade. Pulse until mixture is a uniform texture. Pour onto a plate for easy-access breading.

Smoked Trout Pâté

We buy our smoked ruby red trout from a local fishery. Spread this on little homemade toasts or eat it as a dip with garden vegetables. It dazzles as a brunch item when paired with bagels.

2 smoked trout fillets (the equivalent of
  one whole fish)
4 ounces cream cheese
1 tablespoon fresh lemon juice
1 teaspoon Worcestershire sauce
several good shakes of a hot sauce like Tabasco
2 teaspoons Dijon mustard
⅓ cup toasted pecan pieces
reserve ¼ cup toasted, finely chopped pecans

Peel skin from fish fillets. Flake fish into small pieces and put into the bowl of a food processor. Add the rest of the ingredients (except for the finely chopped pecans) and process mixture until very smooth. If it's too thick, add a tiny splash of half & half or milk and continue to process.

For serving at the restaurant, we scoop out a ball of the pâté with an ice cream scoop, roll it in the finely chopped pecans, and place it on a bed of greens with vegetables and bread decoratively displayed around it.

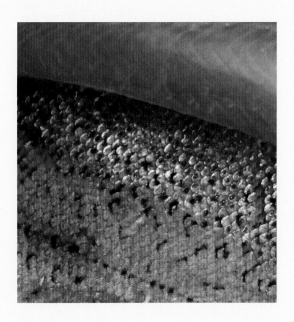

Our Handsome Forager

*To live content with small means; to seek elegance rather than luxury, and refinement rather than fashion;
to be worthy, not respectable, and wealthy, not rich; to listen to stars and birds,
babes and sages, with open heart; to study hard; to think quietly, act frankly, talk gently,
await occasions, hurry never; in a word, to let the spiritual, unbidden and unconscious,
grow up through the common—this is my symphony.*

—WILLIAM HENRY CHANNING, CLERGYMAN, REFORMER (1810–1884)

When we met Breck Crystal, he irreversibly, effortlessly, and almost immediately altered the fabric of our world. It was the middle of our third season. Up to that point we'd known Breck existed—he was the handsome, serious man who worked as a Boulder Outdoor Survival School (BOSS) instructor and lived at Calf Creek Ranch, home of our friend Sara Zorzakis and her two beautiful daughters, Keyera and Makayla. We'd seen Breck in his cowboy hat and buckskin clothes at parties and the post office but didn't know him personally. Then one night Blake dreamt that he suggested a remedy to a health concern she was having. She told us about the dream in the kitchen the next morning, and a few hours later Breck inexplicably appeared at the grill with a jar of acorn-shell tea and some acorn biscotti he'd made. He's been an enormous influence on our lives ever since.

Although he's not an employee and laughs at us when we try to give him money (he lives so sparely that cash appears to be of little use to him), Breck's indispensable to us and to Helles. He's had a tremendous impact on our place-based cuisine philosophy by exposing us to a variety of local wild foods. He drops by the restaurant bringing foraged nettles, cattails, and juniper berries; wild mint that we make into tea; and mustard flowers to sprinkle over trout. And he taught us to process the heirloom rose hips growing in Blake's yard, which we turned into a sauce for seared duck breast. He also makes elk jerky, goat sausage, prickly pear juice, and flour from acorns. In the fall, he hosts a harvest party and a weekend event where he teaches locals about wild foods.

Breck is deeply, profoundly connected to this community and to the wild, isolated land cradling it. Because of his knowledge of even the most far-reaching corners of our stark, relatively uncharted landscape, he's often called upon to participate in search-and-rescue missions to find lost tourists or hikers. He's an inexhaustible resource regarding indigenous and prehistoric knowledge—what we've learned from him cannot possibly be measured. But more than anything else, he's a devoted friend who is, in many ways, personally responsible for our continued love affair with Boulder.

"Breck was a turning point for me in how I experienced Boulder," Jen says. "I was struggling with all its limitations—the ones everyone sees, the ones I fixated on: no stores, no theaters, no music. I wanted more—just something to do with my mind that had no relation to the restaurant. Escape! I found myself at Calf Creek Ranch and was moved by the peace there. I felt fragile from too much work, and Breck let me sit by the fire he fed all day and watch him work. I asked questions, and he explained things in a way that made perfect sense. He taught me to sew using bone tools and sinew, and I made buckskin bags with fringe and twisted straps. I fell in love with Boulder, and it was Breck's fault."

Out of all the human beings we've encountered, Breck is indisputably the most capable. He makes fire from friction and processes game from start to finish (slaughtering, skinning, smoking the hide, then utilizing the entire—and we mean *entire*—animal); he's a total pro at the restaurant, in both the kitchen and the dining room; he's comfortable with any job he's asked to do and provides a solution to every problem thrown at him (he showed Jen the right way to split wood for her drafty, wood-heated cabin and one winter helped fix Blake's furnace when it had all but exploded); he's a natural in the garden, introducing plants like bush mint, mallow, and yarrow. Beyond that, he's our Brecky Poppins, practically perfect in every way, and our patron saint of rejuvenation and healing. He brings us home-brewed chaparral tea and osha root when we're sick and regularly hosts saunas modeled after traditional Native American–style sweat lodges.

Breck has been in Boulder since 1996. "It's one of the hardest places to get to," he says about the town, "and one of the hardest to leave." So true. And he's definitely one reason we haven't left.

Seared Rose Hip Duck

One of the secrets of preparing delicious duck is to cook it only to rare; medium-rare if you must. This keeps the breast moist and tender. Brining the meat in a salt and sugar solution adds flavor and brings a bright freshness.

½ cup kosher salt or ¼ cup table salt
¼ cup sugar
6 duck breasts, skin on
2 tablespoons butter

1. Combine salt and sugar with 1 quart cold water in a medium container. Immerse duck breasts and refrigerate 1 hour to fully season. Remove from brine and pat dry.

2. Poke duck fat with a fork 10 times (be careful not to pierce meat).

3. Melt butter in a large, heavy skillet over medium-high heat. Add duck breasts skin side down and fry until golden, 3 to 4 minutes. Turn with tongs and cook 2 to 3 minutes more.

4. Slice breasts and fan out on plate. Top with rose hip cream sauce with sage.

Rose Hip Cream Sauce with Sage

2 tablespoons butter
4 teaspoons flour
4 tablespoons rose hip powder
I cup red wine
I cup brewed strong black tea (Earl Grey)
2 tablespoons orange juice concentrate
I cup cream
rose hip pieces
8 leaves fresh sage, minced
½ teaspoon salt
⅛ teaspoon cayenne
pinches of ground anise and ground nutmeg

1. Melt butter in small saucepan over medium heat. Add flour and rose hip powder and stir a minute, till fragrant.

2. Whisk in wine, black tea, and orange juice until sauce is smooth and begins to thicken.

3. Whisk in cream and add whole rose hips and sage. Allow to boil very gently for 15 minutes over low heat. The rose hips will soften, and the sauce will reach a rich texture. Add salt and spices; adjust salt to taste.

Pears Poached in Red Wine and Juniper Berries

A beautiful dessert for the fall. It's simple, elegant, and uncommonly delicious. We like to serve the pears whole, standing up in a pool of sauce made from the red wine poaching liquid, with freshly whipped cream and a cinnamon-stick garnish.

2 cups red wine
2 cups water
I cup plus ½ cup sugar
15 juniper berries
3 cinnamon sticks
½ teaspoon salt
6 firm but ripe pears, peeled, with the
    stems attached

1. Combine wine, water, 1 cup sugar, juniper berries, cinnamon sticks, and salt in a saucepan large enough to hold the pears but not so big that the liquid is too shallow.

2. Bring liquid to a boil, stirring now and then to dissolve the sugar. Reduce heat to low and simmer for 5 minutes. Peel pears and trim their bottoms to make a stable base, then set them in the red wine syrup and poach them over low heat for about 10 minutes or until they are just tender. Move them gently, every so often, to make sure they poach evenly.

3. Pour 1 cup of the poaching liquid into a small wide saucepan. Stir in ½ cup sugar and a pinch of salt. Boil the liquid until it has reduced and thickened.

4. Pour a puddle of sauce in the bottom of a glass serving bowl and stand a pear in it. Add a dollop of freshly whipped cream and a cinnamon stick or mint leaf for garnish.

The pears can be cooled and stored in their poaching liquid. They will continue to deepen in color and will keep in the refrigerator for several days.

Gathering Eggs

Love and eggs are best when they're fresh.

—RUSSIAN PROVERB

Farm eggs are the easiest way we've found to convince customers that locally grown, organic foods taste better. One bite and they're ready to go buy their own hen; their eyes roll back in their heads, and they go and book another night at the lodge just so they can come in for breakfast again. They're instant converts. It's almost too easy. Farm eggs are round little miracles wrapped up in beautiful, speckled white and brown shells. They come in all different sizes and are so rich and creamy they make clear why people thought it wise to eat the funny little things in the first place. Another reason farm eggs are so much more delicious is that they're a shade of yellow only nature could invent. It's psychological, perhaps, in the way a red lollipop tastes better than a clear one—who wants to eat a colorless, flavorless, anemic grocery store egg when you could eat one with a yolk the color of mango? Color sends a distinct message to the brain that it's healthy and delicious and ready to be plucked.

"The farm egg is so good," Jen said once, "you almost wish it had matured into a full chicken just so you could eat its leg."

We had a plenitude of local eggs our first year, until a rogue mountain lion came to town and started eating all the hens. Now we have fewer. Our primary local source, Springhill Farm, is certified organic, and we barter with various local farmers for eggs. Bevin McCabe, for example, who owns a llama trekking business in Boulder, trades us eighteen at a time for muffin and coffee breakfasts for her clients. We supplement with cartons from Chino Valley Organics in Arizona once a month as part of our co-op order and store them in refrigerators all over town.

Brian Dick, a trekking guide for Red Rock 'n' Llamas, is one of our many sources for eggs.

Hot Stuff

*Be as wary of a lovely woman as you would be
of a red pepper.*

—JAPANESE PROVERB

Peppers are much more than a central ingredient in the cooking we do every day; they are the soul and spirit of many of our dishes, with the power to transform an ordinary meal into an inimitable culinary sensation. They are, plainly put, our favorite food.

There exist as many varieties of peppers as there do squash and reality television shows. They come big, fat, and green; short, skinny, and bright orange; long and lean and deeply red. And contrary to what many believe, not all are spicy. Of course, some are dangerously so.

Jalapeños, pequins, Anaheim chiles, and poblano chiles grow in our gardens. We roast the fleshy, green poblano chiles on our gas grill and in the oven, then peel them by hand, after which the core is easily pulled out, carrying with it most of the seeds. The remaining seeds are brushed or scraped away. (It's important to remove all the seeds—they'll add a bitter flavor to the dish, make it hotter, ruin the texture, and wreak havoc on your digestive tract. The same goes for the skins, which peel away easily after roasting.) We pair the poblanos with goat cheese as a creamy fettuccine sauce, mix them with jack cheese to fill tamales, or whirl them in a food processor to make poblano crema, the accompaniment to our steak. In early fall we buy big burlap bags of New Mexico's famous Hatch green chiles, which are paler, skinnier, and can be spicier than our peppers. Our secret culinary weapon is the somewhat elusive dried Chimayo chile powder from northern New Mexico. It can be hard to procure but is well worth the effort. With its sweet, bright flavor, it's the perfect match for chocolate. We use it in our signature dessert, the chocolate chile cream pot, and mix it with honey to make our house salad dressing.

If you find yourself with an abundance of jalapeños, it works well to process and freeze them for later use. Begin by rinsing the raw peppers. Slice down the length of the jalapeño, cut off the stem, and scrape away the membrane with a spoon. Then finely chop the jalapeños and store them in an airtight container or bag. To use, carve the amount you need off the frozen pepper block and thaw to make pico de gallo or salsa, or sauté with onion for cream of jalapeño and avocado soup.

She-Devil (Diabla!) Sauce

This is the sauce that will knock your socks off and have you begging for more. It really is hot, no joke. We drizzle it on everything, from quesadillas to burgers to eggs. A bite of yogurt or sour cream can help a burning mouth if you overdo it.

    5 red bell peppers, roasted, peeled, and
      seeded
    2 cloves garlic
    ¼ cup cider vinegar
    ¼ raw onion
    2 teaspoons sugar
    2 teaspoons salt
    2 tablespoons habanero powder

Whirl everything together in a blender until smooth, adding a tablespoon of water if the mixture seems too thick. Make sure there's a window open or an exhaust fan on, as coughing fits from airborne particles can border on the ridiculous.

Keep in a sealed container for up to 10 days.

If using an actual habanero pepper in place of powder, use just 1 pepper and as always, remove stem, seeds, and membrane with protected hands.

We once tried to order habaneros from our suppliers, only to discover that the smallest amount available to us was a whopping 5 pounds!

Sweet Roasted Pepper Dip

This dip is wildly delicious and very simple to prepare. We often serve it with salsa and guacamole as part of a trio of dips for weddings or parties. It goes great with lightly steamed vegetable dippers but is also fabulous on chips, little bread rounds, or new potatoes.

4 cloves garlic
1 teaspoon olive oil
4 red bell peppers roasted, peeled,
    and seeded
½ teaspoon cumin
½ teaspoon dried Chimayo chile powder
5 ounces cream cheese
2 tablespoons sour cream
salt to taste

1. Tightly wrap the garlic cloves and olive oil inside a square of aluminum foil. Place in the oven at 350 degrees for about 45 minutes or until cloves are soft.

2. Squeeze garlic out of peels into the bowl of a food processor or blender.

3. Add red peppers and blend into a puree. Add cumin, chile powder, and cream cheese and blend until the color is even and the texture is smooth.

4. Transfer the mixture to a bowl and stir in sour cream and salt.

Jalapeño and Avocado Cream Soup

Studies show this soup is addictive. When one of our favorite local customers had to have his jaw wired shut to fix a broken bone, his regular request for the duration of his recovery was that we run the soup through the blender and a sieve so he could sip it through a straw. We were more than happy to oblige, because we're enablers.

8 jalapeño peppers, stemmed and seeded
2 tablespoons butter
1 cup finely diced sweet yellow onion
5 cloves minced garlic
8 cups heavy cream
2 cups chopped roasted tomatoes (canned
    fire-roasted tomatoes will work well)
1 cup diced Haas avocado
sea salt and pepper to taste
1 small bunch cilantro, stemmed and
    chopped

1. Mince jalapeños, taking care not to get the chile oils all over your hands, as that has the potential to cause a lot of suffering later.

2. Melt butter in a large, heavy-bottomed pot. Cook finely diced onion and minced jalapeños together in butter over low heat for about 5 minutes, stirring frequently to avoid any scorching. Add minced garlic and continue cooking until onion is translucent and beginning to brown, 20 minutes more.

3. Turn heat to low and add the cream, tomatoes, and avocado. Carefully bring soup to a simmer over low heat. Cook it at a gentle simmer for 30 minutes (a flame tamer is a good bet if you aren't able to keep a close eye on the pot). Stir often to keep soup from sticking.

4. Add generous amounts of salt. (You really have to taste for this. We add a lot, as the cream base can take it, and without salt the subtle flavors of the soup get lost.) Add a good amount of cracked black pepper and most of the cilantro leaves. Garnish the bowls of soup with more cilantro leaves. This soup keeps well and reheats nicely with the help of a flame tamer.

Spicy Cowgal Meat Loaf

Either ground buffalo or beef will work well for this recipe. We buy our grass-fed beef here in Boulder from local ranchers, and it has a distinctive and delicious flavor. It's important to use the best quality, free-range ground meat you can get your hands on.

In one bowl:

2 cups day-old bread, crumbled (we use
    our leftover buttermilk biscuits)
1¼ cups milk
¼ cup mustard
½ cup ketchup (shameless)
½ teaspoon red pepper flakes
I teaspoon crushed Mexican oregano or
    marjoram
I teaspoon ground cumin
I tablespoon salt
I teaspoon black pepper
2 tablespoons Worcestershire sauce
3 pieces chipotle chiles plus I tablespoon
    adobo (the sauce in which they're packed)
2 small onions (2 cups)
3 big cloves garlic
2 red bell peppers roasted, peeled, and
    seeded
2 pounds ground meat
3 eggs

1. Preheat oven to 350 degrees.

2. In a large mixing bowl combine bread, milk, mustard, ketchup, spices, salt, pepper, and Worcestershire sauce. Let bread soak up liquid for 15 minutes.

3. In food chopper (or by hand, chopping into the smallest bits without turning it all to liquid), combine chipotles and adobo, onion, garlic, and red peppers until you have very small pieces.

4. Combine soaked bread crumbs with minced veggies. Add ground meat and eggs. With your fingers, gently squish meat into wet ingredients. Do not overmix! Squeeze and fold until combined. Grease two bread-loaf pans and place half of mixture into each.

5. Cover each meat loaf with greased aluminum foil so they won't stick.

6. Bake for 50 minutes covered, remove foil, and finish baking uncovered for 20 minutes. Internal temperature will reach 160 degrees, and the outside of loaf will be toasty and caramelized. Let cool 1 hour. Work knife around edges and thump out of pans (or serve right out of the pan).

We serve the meat loaf topped with our Backbone sauce and creamed potatoes.

Hint: microwave or fry up a tiny patty of the completed mixture for a taste, to be sure the spicing suits you. Adjust with more salt or a bit of cayenne.

Flourless Chocolate–Chile Torte

This dreamy wheat-free dessert is baked gently in a water bath to keep it creamy and moist. It needs to be cool before cutting but should not visit the fridge until there are leftovers, as the flavors pack a bigger wallop when served at room temperature.

Cake:
2 cups semisweet chocolate chips
1 tablet Mexican chocolate (Abuelita brand)
1 ounce unsweetened chocolate
10 tablespoons butter
2 tablespoons Chimayo chile powder
5 egg yolks
5 egg whites
¼ teaspoon cream of tartar

Topping:
1 cup semisweet chocolate chips
2 tablespoons heavy cream
1 teaspoon honey

1. Heat oven to 350 degrees. Grease and line an 8" cake pan with parchment paper.

2. In heat-proof glass measure, microwave 2 cups chocolate chips, Mexican chocolate tablet, and butter for 2 minutes. Stir and return to microwave until melted, 1 to 2 minutes more. Add Chimayo powder and yolks. If you have no microwave, heat gently in the top of a double boiler over simmering water.

3. Beat egg whites and cream of tartar until they resemble soft peaks. Fold whites ever so gently into chocolate mixture. Pour into prepared pan.

4. Make a water bath: set the 8" pan inside a 12" cake pan (or equivalent) and pour water to reach three-quarters of the way up the side of the chocolate-filled pan. Take care not to get any water in chocolate. Place carefully in oven and bake for 25 to 30 minutes, then remove from oven and remove from bath.

5. Cool cake for 2 hours. Run thin knife along the side of cake and invert onto serving plate. Peel off parchment. Melt together topping ingredients in a heat-proof glass measuring cup for 45 seconds in microwave (or reheat in double boiler). Stir till smooth and pour topping over cake. Spread with a wide spatula or the back of a spoon. Cool 30 minutes.

6. Cut cake into wedges and serve with whipped cream. Garnish with edible flower petals if you want to be like us.

Candied Chile Pecans

These are especially fabulous on mixed greens with our piñon dressing. Make a double batch to serve as a party hors d'oeuvre.

¼ cup vegetable oil
3 tablespoons Kahlua or espresso
1 tablespoon Chimayo chile powder
2 tablespoons sugar
¼ teaspoon salt
2 cups pecan halves

Heat oven to 400 degrees. Combine all ingredients in a small mixing bowl and spread on greased baking sheet. Bake 10 minutes, stir nuts, and return to oven a few minutes more, until fragrant.

One Phone Call:
What We Do When We Need Something

No one is rich enough to do without a neighbor.

—DANISH PROVERB

One obvious difference between the Grill and a lot of other, more accessible restaurants is that when we run out of ingredients, procuring more is nearly impossible. Fortunately, we have good neighbors, and their generosity frequently saves our hides. A standard feature of LDS households is the "pantry." Reminiscent of a bomb shelter, the typical pantry holds enough food to ensure that a family can survive a year of privation. Judi and Larry Davis, thirty-four-year residents of Boulder, have more than a few times bailed us out by letting us raid theirs. We've borrowed maraschino cherries, pecans, bacon, walkie-talkies, and once, when we lost power for two hours with a full dining room and Jen was cooking steaks in the dark, Coleman lanterns.

When the Davises moved to Boulder, only ninety-seven people lived here. Their oldest daughter, Stacy, who has worked for us for four years, was born soon after, bringing the town population to an even hundred. Our first season, when we had no staff and were utterly panicked, Larry and Judi helped by urging their youngest daughter, Jennifer, to apply for a job. She became our first local employee. "It was a blessing for Jennifer to get the job," Judi says. "Blake and Jen were willing to teach her and give her the benefit of their knowledge. They never asked her to do anything contrary to who she is—never expected her to work on Sundays."

From the beginning, Larry and Judi took a parental, caretaking role with us. Our first winter in Boulder, Blake woke to the sound of scraping and found Larry outside shoveling a foot of snow from her walkway. Another time it was freezing, she had run out of heating oil for her furnace, and because of a storm, none would be delivered for a week. She called Judi, who said, "Let me make some calls." Within forty minutes, Blake had been offered five places to stay, and someone brought oil to her. Then there was the time they rescued us in the middle of a winter night when we were bringing groceries back from Richfield, hit a patch of ice, and, while trying to avoid a deer, spun Blake's car into a ditch.

"It was kind of a circus," Larry remembers. "My truck died, the tire was flat…but we felt really honored that we were the ones they called."

Larry and Judi are the people in town who will accommodate the odd weary traveler rolling into Boulder late at night when the lodge is full and there are no vacancies at any local inns. They're the sort of people who won't allow anyone to sleep out in the rain.

Larry is a historian, accomplished woodcarver, romantic (legend has it he once buried poems all over Boulder), flute maker, and former Anasazi State Park Museum director. Judi runs the post office and serves as the town clerk. They're the couple you see taking early morning walks together. And they both share our love of food—particularly food with cultural and historical significance. The Davises frequently host Dutch-oven cookouts for large groups of people. They invite us to Thanksgiving dinner at their home and make it a point to eat dinner at the grill once or twice a month.

"Some old-timers don't go out to eat much," Larry says, "but my jaw was wired shut for almost a year, and Blake and Jen strained their soup for me so I could drink it through a straw. They've always been accommodating. They haven't been pushy. They haven't told people, 'This is the way you should do it because it's better.' They just tried to sit back and understand the mood of the town. They didn't demand anything. We love them, we literally love them. We're glad they're here. We hope they stay. It would be a void if they left."

A Saving Grace

If we could see the miracle of a single flower clearly, our whole life would change.

—BUDDHA

When I first moved to Boulder, Utah, I was sad and lonely. It's strange to admit that now, because at the time my life was rich with experience and friendship. But I was entering my mid-twenties and becoming conscious of the possibilities of myself as a young woman in the world. I had just spent several months working and studying at a Tibetan Buddhist retreat center and had been exposed to profound truths and meditation practices for revealing those truths. I was studying Buddhism with the resident teacher of that community, a Western woman who was trained and ordained by her own teacher, a Tibetan meditation master. My time at the center had been deeply illuminating and transformative, but I still felt very young and inexperienced. I wanted to find my own genuine inspiration for spiritual pursuits. I also wanted to be open to the adventure of life in its myriad forms.

So I came to Boulder with all my girlhood assumptions vanishing before my eyes, and I was terrified of undertaking the profound Buddhist path without deep consideration. I wanted to be sure. And I needed the space to find myself in relationship to that ancient path. The sadness and loneliness came as I realized that my life's direction was up to me and only me. During this period, I longed for my experience to be stripped—exposed to that honest bone. In the sleepy, tiny town of Boulder, I found a chance to sit with all of those possibilities and the implications of whatever I might find. At first I was haunted by the immensity of the lonely desert and canyon country that spread for miles to the south and west. I would certainly die, I felt, if I ventured too far alone in any of the canyons. So I crept out in increments and simultaneously pondered my deepest fears about life and death. Somehow, being out in the open, exposed to the natural elements, became a form of prayer. The desert luridly reminded me that my life was a set of causes and conditions. Also, I began to see clearly that my life wouldn't last, just as the desert was ever changing. Slowly, I became captivated with the vast space surrounding me and the fierce quiet draped all around it.

In between my excursions, I served steaming, scrumptious homemade food to world travelers, American vacationers, and occasional Boulder locals for my friends Jen and Blake at Hell's Backbone Grill. I absolutely adored serving. The simplicity of the act never ceased to fascinate me. I brought hundreds of perfect plates to delighted faces. I liked to imagine that it was more than just food that I was bringing them, and over time I began to realize that it was more. Each plate was a display of the art of mindfulness. The experience nourished in a complete sense. The restaurant environment was always lively and positively glittering with ambience and energy. While my deepest questions and assumptions were falling away, I was infinitely grateful for the wholesome work and great fun. Blake showed me that the perfection of serving could become a powerful expression of my spiritual practice. Jen colored my perceptions with heaps of creative ideas. We danced, wore sparkling outfits, laughed until we fell over, and worked until we were exhausted. Work became the saving grace that lit the way for my internal search.

In my off-hours, I loved the world of no distraction. My home was a little old Chevy Lindy RV adorned with just a few essential belongings, nestled under the shade of a big pine tree and grape arbor. I would sit there, searching for stillness inside, with the stark, vast desert falling in cliff-swoops all around. With this wild, wind-blown space as my backdrop, I examined my innermost questions about life, energy, and purpose. Some days I exerted great effort in contemplation and meditation, as I endeavored to crack open my mind and heart and find a resolute place within myself. The next day I would mimic the desert itself. I would walk in the washes, observe the ancient junipers, and parcel my energy in the most frugal ways. I considered odd, sometimes scary questions. What if my humanity is inconsequential? What if I were to never comb my hair again? What if I die tomorrow? Or even today? I would let the desert wind blow through my hair, let the sand squish between my toes. And the wind blew through me and my ideas of myself.

Reflecting now, I am certain that I found something in Boulder. While I was there, I kept a journal and once wrote down a Buddhist quote that I think of almost daily: "Everything is illusion, but I am confident that all is well." Life continues to be so many things—evocative, sad, compelling, and wildly beautiful. I live now at the same Buddhist retreat center where my journey began. I cook and serve the residents and visiting teachers at our fledgling center. I carry with me the lessons and levity (and some of the recipes) that I learned from Jen and Blake. And I will be forever grateful for my time in Boulder and the place I found within myself.

—ABIGAIL SULLIVAN

Dark Magic Gingerbread

Gingerbread with vanilla ice cream and butterscotch is Blake's favorite childhood dessert. Her version for the restaurant is a very dense and moist cake that uses pears from the historic orchard in Boulder.

3 cups white flour
2 teaspoons baking soda
1 teaspoon salt
3 teaspoons ground ginger
1½ teaspoons cinnamon
½ teaspoon ground cloves
½ teaspoon Chimayo chile
1½ sticks butter
2 eggs
1½ cups sugar
1½ cups dark molasses
1¼ cups boiling water
½ cup diced pear
1 tablespoon chopped crystallized ginger

1. Preheat oven to 350 degrees. Grease and flour a 9 x 13" baking pan.

2. Sift or stir well together the flour, baking soda, salt, and spices.

3. In a large bowl, beat butter until it's creamy. Gradually add eggs and sugar and beat with an electric mixer on high speed until batter is light in color and texture, 2 or 3 minutes. Slowly beat in the molasses.

4. Add flour mixture and stir with a spoon until it's just combined. You don't want to overmix this cake.

5. Stir in boiling water slowly, mixing well, then add diced pear and crystallized ginger.

6. Pour batter into prepared pan and bake it for about 40 minutes or until a toothpick inserted into the middle comes out clean and the cake springs back when lightly pressed on top.

Butterscotch Sauce

This is an old-fashioned favorite. We serve it as one of several toppings for a Fourth of July ice cream social we throw for the town. It is also a crucial component of our ever-popular gingerbread dessert. Butterscotch sauce is similar in ingredients to caramel, another burnt-sugar recipe, but cooked differently.

1 stick unsalted butter
¼ cup water
2 tablespoons light corn syrup
1 cup sugar
½ cup heavy cream
½ teaspoon salt
1 teaspoon vanilla extract or Scotch whiskey

1. Combine butter, water, and corn syrup in a heavy-bottomed saucepan and cook over medium heat, stirring constantly with a wooden spoon until the butter is melted.

2. Add sugar and stir until it's really dissolved—completely smooth and no longer making gritty, scraping sounds.

3. Increase heat and boil without stirring until the mixture starts to brown around the edges. Start stirring at this point, and continue to stir as it thickens and turns a darker brown.

4. When it just barely begins to smoke, remove from heat and pour in cream (be careful here, because it can sputter and get kind of wild). Stir butterscotch until it's dissolved. If it's stubborn and won't melt, place briefly over low heat and stir the lumps out.

5. Add salt and vanilla extract or Scotch and stir well.

This sauce will keep for up to a month in the refrigerator and is great to have on hand. It can be reheated in a microwave or a double boiler.

Chocolate and Black Pepper Bread Pudding

This dessert is extravagant and very rich. It's what we make for BJ's birthday because it's as special as he is. This recipe serves a crowd, but leftovers are what you'll crave at midnight, so go big.

> 1 pound or 4½ cups stale black powder biscuits
> 1 cup heavy cream
> ¾ cup sugar
> ½ teaspoon salt
> 2 cups bittersweet chocolate chips
> 2 ounces unsweetened chocolate
> 2 large eggs
> 2 egg yolks
> 2 cups milk
> 1 tablespoon vanilla extract

1. With your hands, break up the stale biscuits into crumbs and very small chunks.

2. Boil cream with sugar and salt, stirring constantly. Remove from heat, then stir in both kinds of chocolate.

3. Stir until chocolate is melted. Whisk eggs and yolks in a separate bowl, then add milk and vanilla extract to eggs. Combine egg mixture with chocolate liquid, then stir in biscuit chunks.

4. Pour mixture into a generously buttered, 2-quart baking dish. Refrigerate pudding for 2 hours, gently stirring and pressing the bread down into the liquid every now and then.

5. Make a water bath: place the pudding dish inside a larger baking dish in oven and fill outer pan with an inch of water, taking care not to get any water in the pudding.

6. Bake at 350 degrees for about 1 hour or until center is firm to the touch. Remove from oven and water bath. Let pudding cool for 30 minutes.

This pudding can be covered and refrigerated for several days, then reheated in the microwave or oven. We serve it with a sweet whiskey sauce and freshly whipped cream.

Naughty Whiskey Sauce

. . . is to the chocolate bread pudding as satin is to sheets. Sneaking liquor into the sauce was one of our early acts of rebellion.

> 1 stick (8 tablespoons) unsalted butter
> 1 cup sugar
> ¼ cup bourbon (rum and brandy are good alternatives)
> 2 tablespoons water
> ¼ teaspoon salt
> 1 large egg

1. In a heavy-bottomed saucepan, melt butter over low heat. Stir in the sugar, bourbon, water, and salt. Cook, stirring constantly, until sugar is completely dissolved and the mixture is cohesive and well blended. Remove from heat and set aside.

2. Whisk egg until it's frothy, then whisk it with gusto into the hot sugar and liquor. Cook sauce over medium heat, stirring gently until it's simmering. Cook until it thickens (approximately 1 minute). If there are any little lumps, just push the sauce through a strainer.

This sauce will keep for several days in the refrigerator and can be reheated on the stovetop or in a microwave.

Winter

Winter

*Take rest; a field that has rested
gives a bountiful crop.*

—OVID

Boulder winters are so quiet you could take a nap in the middle of the road—if it weren't covered with a foot of snow, that is. No tourists come through town this time of year because many of the roads are impassable, making it even trickier than usual to reach Boulder. In the winter, Boulder epitomizes "sleepy little town." The locals, who customarily squeeze so much work into each day that there's no time left for leisure, are at last forced to slow down. We take it one step further; we don't merely slow down—we come to a full stop. From mid-November to early March, the doors are closed. But before the grand blind-dropping, sign-posting, door-locking, and going-off-for-a-long-winter's-nap ceremony can kick off, Helles must be rocked gently to sleep. As with any young child, that takes some doing.

The garden comes first. It's a job that begins in late fall, when our last crops are past their prime and the gardeners start the somewhat elaborate process of seed-saving. Allowing some crops to go to seed enables us to cull the seeds and use them again the following year. It's a more cost-effective way of gardening but requires some time and effort. When a plant has gone to seed we carefully collect the seed heads or pods and lay them on paper towels for two weeks, until no moisture remains, after which we label and store them in tightly closed glass jars. We save every possible seed for planting in the coming spring. The only kind we haven't had much luck with is squash, which cross-pollinates easily and can result in weird and usually inedible variations. So unless you're interested in mutant pumpkins, it's a bit of a disappointment.

Next on the list is to remove everything from the garden. The gardeners till the soil and plant cover crops like legumes, buckwheat, and vetches to add organic matter and fix nitrogen into the soil. They cut any remaining flowers so we can use them as garnish and harvest the last of the herbs, which we dry. Drying herbs concentrates their flavor. (When substituting dried herbs in recipes calling for fresh, reduce your dose. Our general rule is one teaspoon of crumbled, dried herbs for every tablespoon of fresh, chopped herbs.) Drying herbs is not labor intensive, but the sifting, sorting, cleaning, and separating will occupy a good couple of afternoons that might otherwise be spent doing yoga or watching *Sex and the City* reruns on video. One garbage bag of fresh herbs yields approximately one large Zip-Loc of dried, but if you have the time and the floor or counter space, it's more than worth it. "The first time I dried herbs," Jen says, "I had pictured cute, tiny bundles hanging in front of my windows, perfuming my house. Instead I had a big mess in my living room."

The process of drying herbs is similar to that of saving seeds. Spread them out on paper towels (or sheets, if you're drying in bulk), turning them every few days. Herbs tend to dry at different rates. Thyme, for instance, will dry in just a few days, whereas parsley can take a full week. It depends on the temperature and humidity in your home. A temperature of about eighty-five degrees is best, with humidity below 60 percent.

The last step in putting the garden to sleep is to "overwinter" it, which involves burying the garden and any remaining living plants, like carrots or beets, in straw mulch. It will lie dormant during the winter, until we uncover it in March, dig up the carrots, and start fresh.

At the end of the season, Blake sits down with the gardener to map out the garden for the following season and take stock of what seeds we have available and what we need to order. We purchase seeds from the High Altitude Seed Trust, Native Seeds/SEARCH, Seeds for Change, Peaceful Valley, and Planet Natural. All these companies offer organic seeds. Native Seeds/ SEARCH carries a variety of regional southwestern plants and heirloom varieties.

With the business of the garden checked off the list, we only have to clean the restaurant, an operation that doubles as a party: loud, loud music—so loud everyone has to yell to ask where the extra Citrasolv is kept, or what should be done with the purple feather boa someone just found in the closet. We finally address the teetering piles of notes, recipes, Polaroids (many taken by BJ of Tashi sitting at the table with various and sundry people), and old grease-spattered menus. We dole out any food that won't keep for five months and take inventory. Then. (Drum roll.) We close the blinds, hang the sign, lock the doors, and *Just Walk Away, Renee.*

Hibernation, relaxation. Time holds still in Boulder as layers of sparkling snow cover the ground and mountains. The thick, square buttes come to look like giant blocks of vanilla ice cream. The stillness and silence are astonishing. Like everyone else in town, we've stockpiled food and firewood. Now we sleep in, take two hours to drink our morning coffee, stay in our pajamas till

Top left: Preparing Dutch-oven delights. Bottom left: Sun-dried tomatoes from our end-of-season surplus. Top right: A post-Thanksgiving wild turkey sighting in downtown Boulder. Bottom right: The "Hogsback," connecting Boulder to Escalante, is considered one of the most scenic drives in America.

Bob, Sioux, and their boys, Ry, Cru, and Dawz, in the barn at Boulder Mountain Ranch off Hell's Backbone Road.

midday. We have time to play canasta with Breck and BJ; visit our families; travel to New Mexico, Arizona, and California; and finally call our friends in other towns to reassure them that we haven't been run over by a tractor.

Like fishermen who spend their winters repairing nets, we spend our winters readying ourselves for the coming season, answering long-overdue correspondence, organizing, making repairs to the kitchen equipment, laying in a stock of supplies. Throughout the months, we continue to make improvements to the grill. But otherwise, we try our best to shed our restaurant skins. The only cooking we do is for ourselves and friends who drop by—roasted chicken and veggies or deep, hearty pots of posole. We accept every dinner invitation that comes our way, giving others the chance to cook for us. And we realize with fantastic clarity how disconnected our lives become from our families and our friends during the cruel nine-month schedule of the season, when the boundaries between work and life barely exist. Winter reminds us that we do have a life. In an agrarian, rural community such as this one, everything turns inward in the winter—there are few out-of-town visitors. Instead, the community reconnects. People host dinner parties, cook, and bake for one another.

Not everyone stays home, though. Many locals take advantage of the slow winter to travel—the Cochrans, Bob, Sioux, and their boys Ry, Cru, and Dawz, 15, 13, and 11, for example. The Cochrans are cattle ranchers; they own the 160-acre Boulder Mountain Ranch and run an outfitting business leading tourists on horseback through Utah's backcountry. They've taken us horseback riding, and their son Ry is one of our dishers. In the winter, the Cochrans hang a sign across the gate at Boulder Mountain Ranch that says, "Gone Surfin'," then the hardworking cowboy family trades in boots for flip-flops, throws surfboards in the back of their pickup, and heads to the beaches of Mexico.

Us, we rest. We sit and read, do crafts, savor the long, unoccupied afternoons. Jen bakes and cooks to warm her house. We watch movies. Time passes slowly. It's a funny, old-fashioned life we lead in the winter, but it's authentic. It's our reward for working hard the rest of the year. And if we've learned anything from our time in Boulder, we've learned bedrock survival—if you want to survive, you work as hard and as well as you possibly can. Because it makes all the rest that much more beautiful.

How'd Ya Ever Find This Place?

We truly are in the middle of nowhere, but at the same time it feels like the vortex of the world, because uncannily, all we need to survive eventually comes here to us. Over the years, our customers have become our lawyers, dentists, chiropractors, hairdressers, meat suppliers, and employees.

The arrival of Tomalene Evans in Boulder is a prime example of how serendipitous circumstances preserve the well-being of little Helles. Tomalene, a server at the grill, wins the prize for best answer to the Number-One Question Our Customers Ask: "How'd ya ever find this place?"

"I was on a mountain-biking trip for a week and a half, and I went this way because I'd heard it was more scenic," Tomalene remembers. "Halfway across Nevada, my clutch started making funny noises. At Calf Creek Ranch on Highway 12, the clutch blew out and my truck died."

With the help of two campers, Tomalene nursed her truck to the side of the road, popped her bike off the roof, and rode it over the Hogsback and into lower Boulder.

"It was my first time going over the Hogsback, and it was astonishing. I was dodging RVs, and I rode straight to the grill. I was drawn in by the look and feel of the place—it was calm and comforting, and I needed somewhere to sit and have a cup of tea and contemplate my newfound situation."

Tomalene did her contemplating on the grill's redwood deck, beside the fishpond full of cattails and beneath the prayer flags and hummingbird feeders. While she ate fresh coffee cake and drank a cup of tea, she asked her waitress, Jennifer Davis, what it was like to live in Boulder. "She told me she'd grown up here and that it was wonderful, and if I was interested in sticking around I should come back and talk to Blake. I had to have my truck towed to St. George, which put me in Boulder for a week with my bike. By the end of the week, I was madly in love with the town and the restaurant and Blake and Jen."

When her truck was fixed, Tomalene drove back to Oregon, where she was living at the time, packed her things, and within a week turned around and headed back to Boulder.

123

Wicked Hot Chocolate

A very grown-up version of an old standard, with Chimayo chile and cinnamon adding considerably to the warming effect.

½ cup unsweetened cocoa powder
2 ounces unsweetened chocolate
½ cup sugar
3 cinnamon sticks
2 teaspoons Chimayo chile powder
½ teaspoon salt
5 cups whole milk
½ cup half & half
1 teaspoon vanilla extract

1. Mix cocoa, sugar, chile, and salt into a small bowl.

2. In a medium saucepan, stir milk, half & half, and cinnamon sticks over low heat until mixture comes to a simmer.

3. Whisk in cocoa mixture and cook until cocoa is smooth and an even color and consistency. Add vanilla extract.

We serve the hot chocolate in a big mug, topped with whipped cream, a cinnamon stick, and chocolate shavings.

Milk Bread

Sometimes we make plain white bread for the back of the house as total comfort food—a thick slice covered in butter and rock salt makes everything all right. Kneading this dough on a lightly greased rather than floured surface will yield better results, and baking it free-form gives a nice, rustic touch.

1 package yeast (or scant teaspoon)
⅓ cup warm water
3 cups flour
2 teaspoons salt
2 tablespoons sugar
½ cup milk
½ cup hot water
¼ cup melted butter

1. In large mixing bowl, dissolve yeast in water. Add remaining ingredients; stir until dough comes away from sides of bowl. On the counter, knead by hand until smooth, about 8 minutes.

2. Form dough into a ball and let it rise in a greased bowl in a warm place, covered, for 1 hour.

3. On the counter, shape risen dough into log and press into greased loaf pan. Flip out and replace, so the smooth bottom of dough is now the top. Cover and let rise in pan for 60 minutes, until bread crests sides of pan.

4. Bake for 35 minutes at 350 degrees. Let cool in pan 5 minutes, then remove from pan and cool at least 30 minutes before cutting.

Marry-Me Cornbread

A plumped-up version of our everyday cornbread muffins, so delicious it inspires wedding proposals. It's a meal in itself.

5 pieces bacon cut into ½" strips
I cup onion, chopped
2½ cups yellow cornmeal
1¾ cups flour
I cup brown sugar
I teaspoon baking soda
I teaspoon salt
I tablespoon baking powder
2 eggs
½ cup oil
2½ cups milk or buttermilk
I can creamed corn
8 ounces packaged cream cheese,
    cut in ½" chunks

1. Heat oven to 350 degrees. On stovetop in 12" cast-iron skillet, fry bacon and onions till onions are translucent.

2. In large mixing bowl, stir together cornmeal, flour, brown sugar, baking soda, salt, and baking powder until well combined. Stir in eggs, oil, milk, and creamed corn. Pour into hot skillet and gently mix into onions and bacon.

3. Dot top of cornbread with cream cheese chunks and bake 30 to 40 minutes, until top is golden and springs back when touched. Serve in warm wedges.

Brown Sugar Blue Cornbread

Crumble a sweet wedge of this delight into red chile posole or bake it in muffin tins and serve with whipped butter. And there was great rejoicing . . .

2½ cups blue cornmeal
1¾ cups flour
I cup brown sugar
I teaspoon baking soda
I teaspoon salt
I tablespoon baking powder
2 eggs
½ cup (I stick) melted butter or oil
I tablespoon butter
2½ cups milk

1. Heat oven to 350 degrees. Warm a 12" cast-iron Dutch oven in oven for 10 minutes while you assemble the batter.

2. In a medium bowl, combine the cornmeal, flour, brown sugar, baking soda, and salt. Stir in eggs, melted butter, and milk. Batter will be thick.

3. Remove heated skillet from oven, add 1 tablespoon butter, and swirl it around to coat surface. Pour batter into buttered Dutch oven, spreading it around evenly. Return skillet to oven and bake 45 minutes, till sides of cornbread pull away from Dutch oven.

Delicious additions:
2 cups grated cheese, 3 tablespoons minced jalapeños, 1 cup diced red peppers, 1 cup roasted corn, or ½ cup chopped green chiles.

Brown Betty Granola

Our house granola is the creation of our beloved kitchen manager Colleen. This breakfast staple full of flaxseed and almonds keeps us deliriously happy, morning after morning. One recipe makes a nice big batch—store extra in airtight containers.

8 cups rolled oats
2 cups bran
½ cup sesame seeds
I cup coconut
2 cups sliced almonds
I cup flaxseed
I tablespoon cinnamon
½ teaspoon salt
¾ cup maple syrup
½ cup canola oil
½ cup honey
I tablespoon vanilla extract

1. Heat oven to 350 degrees. In a large bowl combine oats, bran, sesame seeds, coconut, almonds, and flaxseed. Sprinkle cinnamon over top of mixture.

2. In a saucepan gently heat salt, maple syrup, oil, honey, and vanilla extract till thin, about 5 minutes. Pour over oat mixture and stir well to be sure oat mixture is well coated.

3. Spread mixture onto sprayed or parchment-lined pans. Bake at 350 degrees for 12 minutes, turning granola with a wide spatula, then baking for another 5 to 10 minutes, until golden brown and fragrant. Let cool and store in airtight containers.

Blue Corn Flapjacks

Blue corn originated with the Hopi tribe, who reside in northern Arizona. These pancakes are fluffy, sweet, and very satisfying. People eat them and freak out.

3 cups flour
I cup sugar
I tablespoon baking powder
I teaspoon salt
I cup blue cornmeal
4 eggs
3 cups milk
½ cup oil
I teaspoon vanilla extract
more oil for greasing griddle

1. In a large mixing bowl combine flour, sugar, baking powder, salt, and cornmeal.

2. In another bowl, lightly beat eggs with milk, oil, and vanilla extract.

3. Add wet to dry and combine well.

4. Preheat griddle to medium-hot. A drop of water will dance over the griddle when it's ready. Grease by pouring 2 tablespoons oil on it and spread around with a folded paper towel. Keep the folded paper towel on standby to grease the griddle for the next batch of cakes.

5. Pour from a pitcher or use a ladle to make standard round cakes, or get wacky and make a portrait pancake for each breakfast companion. Turn cake when edges are set and small bubbles form and pop on the surface.

The batter will keep in the fridge for two days.

Alternate taste sensation

Cinnamon Graham Griddle Cakes

In place of the blue cornmeal, add 1 cup graham cracker crumbs and 1 teaspoon cinnamon.

The Amazing Tortillas of Gloria Hallelujah

No mean woman can cook well. It calls for a generous spirit, a light hand, and a large heart.

—PAUL GAUGUIN

Gloria Arochi is responsible for many of the south-western-influenced flavors on the menu; she's integrated into our kitchen what she learned growing up in Nogales, Mexico. She's also the miraculous big sister young Helles needed in order to survive her somewhat unorthodox, rebellious adolescence. Affectionately known as Gloria Hallelujah, she is, hands down, our favorite action figure—one tiny woman capable of the work of four men and a Hobart mixer. When Gloria opens up the back door during prep time, walks in, and calls out her loud and cheerful hello ("Coffee!!"), a whole kitchen of women look up from their bowls or sinks and heave a collective sigh of relief, grateful in advance for the sleight of hand she's about to pull. No matter how far behind we are on prep work or how close we are to giving up and abandoning Helles (and being labeled deadbeat parents for the rest of our lives), Gloria invariably rescues us. We hug her, give her coffee, and let her throw on an apron and go about her business. One of those rare and invaluable employees who require virtually no instruction, she intuits what needs to happen in the kitchen and just goes for it.

"I usually get to the restaurant and just see what needs to be done," she says. "If something needs to be done, I do it. I make the tortillas and the salsa. I peel potatoes, make the bread."

Gloria can be held fully accountable for the pain inflicted on heedless customers who allege to "like it hot" and then, despite solemn warnings, enthusiastically spoon she-devil hot sauce all over their unsuspecting organic farm eggs. It's the best they've had in their lives, they declare through tears, their voices a bit high-pitched and hysterical. Gloria hand-forms all our tamales, which we then fill with roasted poblano peppers and Cotija and jack cheese. She also heads up all flour tortilla production.

Herein lies, quite possibly, her most remarkable superpower: her homemade flour tortillas. They are truly a thing of ineffable mystery and beauty. She makes them, and we whistle and hop and stomp our feet and clap loudly—at least inwardly. The fact is, we can make tortillas ourselves—Blake used to do them and they were great—big, fat, red chile or red pepper gorditas made one by one. But the twelve tortillas she'd produce in a day would be depleted after only six quesadillas were sold, and she'd

have to start all over again. Enter Gloria Hallelujah, the greatest one-woman show in our galaxy. She fills each request: red chile, roasted red pepper, green chile, thin and huge, small and fat. She handles the task deftly, generating dozens of tortillas in a single session. And then, whenever she leaves town on vacation, we silently, covertly remove all traces of them from the menu—we don't even bother trying to fake it, because at this point people are so addicted that we'd be revealed as imposters and possibly hanged in effigy from our deck. So until she returns, no more smoked trout and sharp white cheddar quesadilla appetizers. No egg, crumbled bacon, and cheese quesadillas on our Mini-Me kid's menu. No green chile and jack quesadillas, no calabacitas or squash-blossom quesadillas. Nothing. No quesadillas for you! If you want quesadillas, you go find Gloria, tell her to come back.

Gloria remembers being in the kitchen with her mother and sisters at seven or eight years old, peeling and chopping. Now

Gloria Arochi and her sister Chely hand-form tamales. The duo has been known to form and tie two hundred tamales in a single session.

she's passing on that tradition. "One thing I love," she says, "is that I can bring my kids with me to the restaurant."

Gloria has seven children, all of whom have, in one capacity or another, worked at the grill. Her youngest, America, who is seven years old, can quite competently wield a kitchen knife, make chocolate-chip cookies, operate our industrial dishwasher, and make a perfect cup of coffee for her mother, with exactly the right amount of cream and sugar. America has quite a future at the grill. "I like going to the restaurant because I get to wash dishes and help my mommy squash potatoes," America says. "And I get paid with root beer and orange juice and pancakes. I like going there because I can help other people, like Jen and Blake. They're always nice to me."

Gloria says she appreciates working for Buddhists. "I respect their beliefs, and one thing I've really learned is forgiveness and to control my anger. It carries over into how I deal with my kids. I think about that, and when my kids make me angry, I try to calm down. In my home life, I experiment to see what happens. I don't know too much about Buddhism, but I experiment and see what happens, and sometimes it works."

She has been in the United States since 1992. "This is the best job I've ever had," she says. "I have a lot of hardship in my life, and it's a kind of medicine here for me. I feel happy at the grill. It's a good place to come to. When I started working here, I never even thought about the pay. I just wanted to come because Blake and Jen were so nice to me. When you feel special, you can make more space for yourself. They make space for me; Jen always has a counter cleared and ready for me to work. This feeling is really strong for me. I've learned a lot from this experience, to find and know people who are really open and accepting. These two wonderful, crazy women have helped me to trust."

A tamale in progress, filled with red chile, local lamb, and garden mint.

Green Chile Corn Tamales

This is a combination of two recipes from our two favorite tamale makers: Jen's grandma and our friend Martha Clark. Best results are achieved when ingredients are combined in a stand mixer with the paddle attachment. Yields about 5 dozen tamales.

> I pound softened butter
> 5-pound bag prepared masa (found in refrigerator section) or 8 cups dry masa harina, plus 4 cups water to moisten into dough
> 2 teaspoons baking powder
> 2 teaspoons salt
> 2 ears corn, roasted under broiler or on grill till golden, then scraped off the cob
> 2 cups green chiles, roasted, peeled, and chopped
> corn husks (*hojas*)
> I pound pepper jack cheese, cut into logs ½ x 3"

1. Soak corn husks in warm water until soft, rinse thoroughly.

2. Beat butter about 3 minutes, till light in color. Add wet masa, baking powder, and salt to butter and beat 20 minutes. When it's ready, a chunk of masa dropped in a glass of water will float. Beat in the corn and chiles.

3. Open husk flat on the table with wide end toward you. Spread husk with about 2 tablespoons masa, lay cheese down the middle, fold sides in, then bring the top end toward you. A pretty touch: tear extra corn husk into strips and tie one loosely around the tamale to hold the top flap down.

4. Steam the tamales by placing them standing on end, open end up, on a rack in a large steamer or pressure cooker. Steam for 45 minutes or pressure cook for 20 minutes at 15 pounds pressure.

5. Let tamales rest 15 minutes before digging in. Top with pure red chile sauce.

Hallelujah Quesadilla

Quesadillas are a favorite appetizer at the grill, as well as the most requested employee meal. They are simply folded-over flour tortillas stuffed with cheese, chiles, and other goodies, then toasted till crisp and golden.

An essential ingredient is, of course, cheese (*quesadilla* is American Spanish, a diminutive of *quesada*, a type of cheesecake, from *queso*, cheese). Choose a cheese that melts easily and will complement rather than compete with the other flavors in your quesadilla. You may choose to fill your creation with grilled or shredded meats, raw or roasted vegetables, or simply chiles and cheese. Add sour cream, guacamole, or our she-devil sauce as a final accompaniment.

If you're lucky, you might have the chance to buy handmade flour tortillas from a local cook or restaurant in your town. Buy a dozen and wrap and freeze what you won't be using. Commercial tortillas can be delicious: look for those made with fewer ingredients and check expiration dates on packages.

We often grill our quesadillas on the barbecue over a low flame to get the attractive markings and that smoky taste, but it's easy to overstuff them,* so a pan-cooked quesadilla retains anything that may otherwise ooze out. You will need a skillet and lid the same diameter or larger than your tortilla.

1. Lightly oil skillet and heat over medium flame.

2. Lay tortilla in heated skillet. Sprinkle ingredients over one-half of tortilla. Fold the empty half over to cover the filling. Cover and cook on medium heat about 3 minutes.

3. Turn the quesadilla over to toast what was the top. This will take just 2 to 3 minutes more. Both sides will be crispy and golden.

4. With a spatula, remove from skillet to cutting board. Let sit 1 minute to give the cheese a chance to cool for cutting. Slice and enjoy.

Note that too much cheese sounds like a good idea until it glops out all over everything. Use no more than ½ cup grated cheese per 12" tortilla.

Some of our favorite flavor combinations

- Smoked trout and sharp white cheddar cheese

- Sautéed summer squash, green chile, fresh corn, and jack cheese

- Roasted red bell pepper and goat cheese

- Grilled chicken, green chile, and pepper jack cheese

- Arugula pesto and havarti cheese

- Scrambled eggs, bacon crumbles, and cheddar cheese

The LeFevre Family

Trees are not known by their leaves, nor even by their blossoms, but by their fruits.

—ELEANOR OF AQUITAINE (1122–1204)

"Boulder's a great place to raise kids. If I didn't live in Boulder, I wouldn't have adopted these kids." Gladys LeFevre is perched on the edge of a piano bench in the living room of the farmhouse where she and her husband, Dell, the Garfield County commissioner, live with their children. It's the original Lyman homestead, built in Boulder in 1889. Gladys, Miss Garfield County 1964 and a former town council member, is the granddaughter of Boulder's first settler. Both Gladys and Dell were born and raised in Boulder and lived elsewhere for much of their lives. They bought the old Lyman ranch in 1965, the first year they were married, and moved back to town ten years later.

For Gladys to say she wouldn't have adopted the children if she lived elsewhere is significant when you consider how many there are: fourteen, ten of whom currently live at home. The two oldest are American boys of Hispanic descent, and the girls all come from India except Marina, who at nine years old is the youngest. She's from Colombia. Their two youngest sons are from Bolivia. "We have five bathrooms," Dell says, "and we need five more."

Gladys and Dell have dedicated a tremendous amount of their lives to raising their children carefully and are cautious when it comes to the places the kids are allowed to work. But they've demonstrated trust in us by allowing not one but five of their daughters to work at the grill. Aruil, Anna, Amelia, Ellayna, and Sieta have all been or are employees. They wash dishes, prep food, and back up the servers when they're busy, making desserts and salads. They're fast, efficient, and incapable of complaint. And they make us laugh really, really hard. Even Gladys puts in time at the grill, showing up to wash dishes voluntarily when one of her daughters is scheduled to work but can't make it.

"I appreciate the fact that they get to work for someone besides me. I tell them, 'You stick with Blake and Jen, you're going to learn some skills, so that when you go to college you'll be able to get a job,'" Gladys says. "That's why I go down to work at the restaurant. I tell the girls, 'We have to keep our place there. If you guys are sick or something and there's nobody to go to work, I'll go and fill in.'"

"I think there's still a lot of kid in both Blake and Jen, so they're able to relate to the kids in a way others might not be able to," Dell adds. "Sometimes somebody else can have more influence than you can as a parent."

Dell LeFevre is one of Boulder's most established, respected, and colorful old-school cattle ranchers. He started ranching at the age of twelve, and today he epitomizes the part: big hat, faded jeans, worn boots, and a low, gravelly voice that goes a mile a minute, always challenging you to guess whether he's being deeply serious or completely pulling your leg.

"Thirty years ago," he says, "there were just cowmen and the power plant job here. There aren't many old-timers left in Boulder, and sometimes, after a day on the highway, I don't know what I'm still doing here." But for all his talk, it's doubtful he's going anywhere. Not with ten kids in Boulder to take care of, fifteen cats, about twenty horses, five hundred cows, and a dog.

When Gladys and Dell were children growing up, Boulder was a cattle and dairy town, the cash crops being milk, cheese, and cream. The roads in and out of town weren't yet paved, and once a year Gladys went with her family to Richfield to get the year's supply of groceries and visit the dentist. "It was over dirt roads," she remembers, "too far to travel in those conditions but once a year." Richfield is now an easy, well-paved two-hour drive from Boulder. And because it's the site of the nearest Kmart, Krispy Kreme, and small-animal veterinarian, someone's usually heading that way every few weeks.

"I think you have to learn to accept change," Gladys says. "If you sit back and say, 'Hey, I refuse to change,' you'll become extinct. There's a certain amount of progress bound to happen. What are you going to do? You can kick and scream all you want, but if there's a demand and a need for something, it changes. And you have to make the best of it. We'd all like to have the road oiled over the mountain, and we'd like to roll it up behind us when we come over it and then roll it out again when we go out."

One day last fall Dell came into the restaurant. "Bishop talked about my girls in church today," he said. Well, duh, we thought; put all his daughters together and that's a fair percentage of the town's population. They're going to turn up in sermons from time to time. "I sat up straight and listened because he was talking about my girls," Dell said.

From left to right: Ellayna, Anna, Gladys, Aruil, Sieta, Amelia.

But Dell wasn't referring to his daughters at all—he meant us. The bishop had brought to the congregation a copy of *O, The Oprah Magazine*, which included a feature article about us and the restaurant. The article had been published earlier that week, and we'd felt some trepidation about the community's response; it focused heavily on our early days in Boulder when we were struggling to find employees and acquire a liquor license. But

the bishop had declared the article good for the town, favorable press for Boulder. "I was proud of my girls," Dell said, beaming at us, standing there in the dining room.

But there was no way in Hell's Backbone he was half as proud as we were, hearing that the bishop approved of us—and hearing Dell call us his girls.

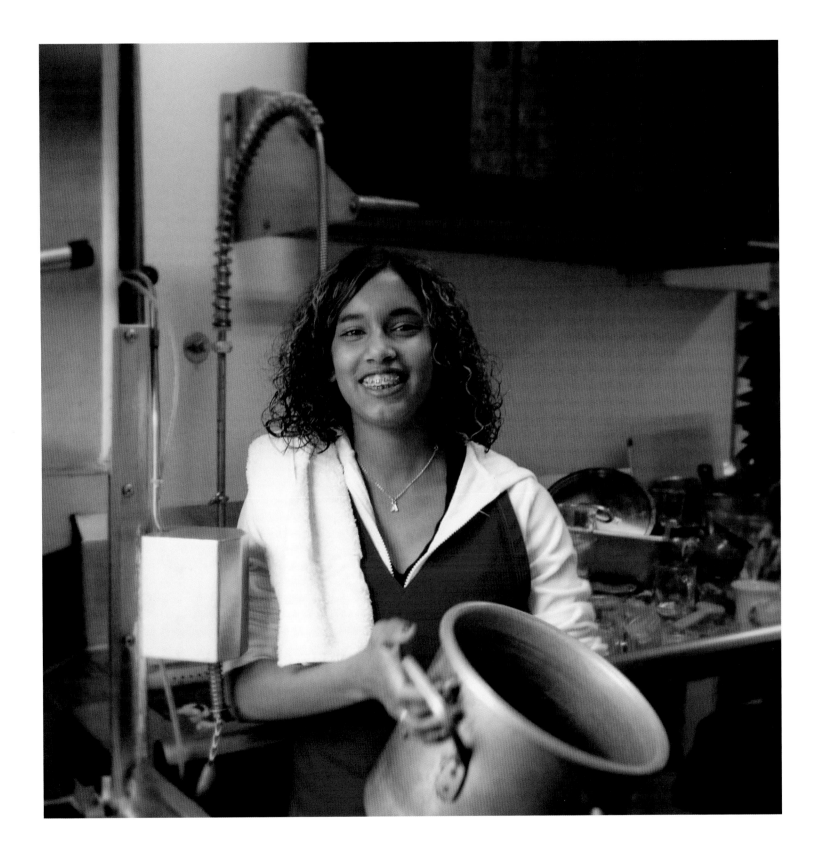

Growing Up in Our Kitchen

Praise the young and they will blossom.

—IRISH PROVERB

Most restaurants have an office, and somewhere in that office sits a thick stack of applications—old, surplus applications accepted the last time the restaurant placed an ad in the newspaper and routinely turned away all who didn't quite make the cut. Perhaps the applicants had logged fewer than four years fine-dining experience or failed to correctly name a wine that could be paired with lamb.

Oh, if it were only that easy for us. We don't have a stack of applications in our office from people who saw our ad in a newspaper, because, well, for one thing, we don't have an office, and for another, we don't have a newspaper. We take a relatively different approach to finding employees. We joke that we'll hire anyone with a pulse, but more accurately, we'll hire anyone with a good heart. A lot of the time that comes in the form of local kids—high school or college students who are ready to have a job and whose parents have agreed to let them work for us. As a result, we're probably the only Zagat-rated restaurant in America with so many employees working their first-ever restaurant job. Unlike other restaurateurs, experience isn't paramount to us; in fact, it's barely a consideration. What impresses us most is work ethic, willingness, and good manners, the characteristics we believe make good employees. And surprisingly, when "experience required!" is eliminated from the hiring process and you're forced to look beyond what an applicant has done to what you think he or she can do, often the rewards are much greater.

It would be a task to find someone we adore quite as completely as we do our beautiful little Amelia "Bedelia" LeFevre. A junior in high school now, Amelia has worked at the grill for three seasons and seems to be growing up in the kitchen in front of our eyes. She's the perfect teenage sidekick—she experiments with glitzy makeup and fashion and has as insatiable a thirst for girltalk as we do. She's known at the grill for her speed and hard work, for her inexhaustible curiosity (every shift, she asks at least one smart, thought-provoking question, some of which we have to pretend to know the answers to), and for turning red as a Chimayo chile, laughing nervously, and replying, "Whatever!" to any compliment she receives. Of course this only eggs us on.

"We're like friends with the bosses," Amelia says. "It's not like a boss-employee relationship. You can hang out and have fun."

It's a Sunday night, the restaurant has just closed, and Amelia's in the dining room, taking a break from washing the remaining few dishes. She keeps glancing furtively at the kitchen door, as if it's giving her an ulcer to leave a colander and three cruets in the sink for a few minutes. This is the first job she's ever had, which is a total shocker when you witness her in action—she's a little machine; a wind-up toy in Dishland.

"I don't know how it would be working for anyone else," Amelia says. "I've learned how to work and be responsible here. Blake and Jen expect a lot out of me. It makes me want to do a good job—I like going away from my job knowing they're happy with me. It gives me a good feeling inside."

Of course we've given Amelia a code name. (No one is safe—everyone gets renamed working for us.) To the rest of Boulder, Utah, she's Amelia LeFevre—but to us she'll always be Tiny Dancer. It took years, but we think she might finally be cured of the horrific torture she initially felt when we urged her to dance with all of us while we closed. It's part of the job, we'd tell her, dancing around the dining room to Destiny's Child. It's part of the plan.

"They're young and fun," Amelia says. "They love to turn the music up and dance and act crazy. It's not all serious all the time—but I like how they're serious when they need to be. Whenever they drive me home, they always tell me what a good job I've done. And Blake's always giving everyone hugs. At first I thought, 'This is my boss giving me a hug,' but now I feel like they're part of my family. It can be a place for me to come when I want to forget about the rest of the world. And I like learning about Blake's Buddhism. I'll hear Blake talking about her God, and it's okay."

Amelia's quiet for a few seconds before she speaks again. "I think everyone should have an experience with bosses like Blake and Jen—the kind of bosses who are more like friends. I'm sixteen now, and I've worked here three seasons. If they stay here until I graduate, I'll work here until I graduate."

(We consider this a verbal, binding contract and are contemplating legal action if Amelia attempts to leave us before graduating from high school.)

Christmas Posole

Jen's childhood Christmases had visions of posole dancing in her head. While there are innumerable variations on the theme of corn, meat, and chile, this very southwestern hominy stew represents the flavors you'll taste at a New Mexican holiday supper. It's made in stages, and the preparation takes several hours. Start it early in the day or the day before you need it to give yourself enough time and to allow the flavors to get friendly; it's always better after it sits a few hours.

> 1 pound posole corn (dried, lime treated),
>   rinsed, plus 10 cups water*
> 2 pounds pork shoulder plus 8 cups water
> 1 onion cut in half, studded with 6 whole cloves
> 2 stalks celery
> 3 cloves garlic
> 1 tablespoon dried or 2 sprigs fresh thyme
> 1 tablespoon peppercorns
> 1 tablespoon red pepper flakes
> 2 tablespoons canola oil
> 2 onions, diced
> 4 stalks celery, diced
> 2 tablespoons salt
> 2 teaspoons Mexican oregano or marjoram
> 1 tablespoon cumin
> 1 teaspoon coriander
> 4 cloves garlic, minced
> red chile sauce (recipe follows)

1. Place posole corn and 10 cups water in a large stewing pot. Bring to boil on high heat.

2. Reduce heat to low and simmer for 4 to 5 hours, till posole "pops" open, stirring every half hour. Add more water if necessary.

3. In a large stockpot, combine pork, 8 cups water, halved, studded onion, celery stalks, cloves of garlic, thyme, peppercorns, and red pepper flakes. Cook on medium heat for 3 hours, covered, with lid ajar. Add more water as needed to keep meat immersed; you're also creating the soup's base.

4. Meat is ready when it flakes apart easily. Remove pork from stockpot to a large bowl. Strain pork broth into the posole corn stewing pot, combining the two. Set to low simmer. When cool enough to handle, flake the meat in large chunks and add to the stew pot.

5. In a 10" cast-iron skillet, fry onion and celery in oil until soft. Add salt, Mexican oregano, cumin, coriander, and garlic and cook 1 minute more.

6. Add batch of red chile sauce, stir it up, and cook 3 minutes.

7. Pour the skillet of red chile into stew pot. Combine all the ingredients and let simmer 2 hours. Adjust salt to taste.

Serve posole with tortillas or cornbread, allowing guests to top their own bowl with grated cheese, fresh cilantro, sour cream, avocado, or lime wedges.

Canned white hominy will do in desperate times. This substitution saves many hours, but the flavor and texture are inferior.

Red Chile Sauce

Jen grew up in New Mexico. Chile is serious. Pure red chile is the perfect side for tamales, the base for enchiladas and posole, and guaranteed to stain everything it comes into contact with. A softer-skinned chile like the pasilla eliminates the need for straining the sauce.

> 10 to 15 dried red chile pods (stems broken
>   off, seeds dumped out)
> 6 cloves garlic
> 2 teaspoons salt
> 1 teaspoon cumin
> 1 teaspoon Mexican oregano
> reserved water from the chile soaking pot

1. In a pot, cover pods with water and bring almost to a boil. Turn off heat, stir, and steep 10 minutes.

2. In a blender, combine chile pods, spices, and chile water, filling blender to the halfway mark with liquid. Blend on medium-high for 5 minutes.

Scotty Mitchell

"What is art? Nature concentrated."

—HONORÉ DE BALZAC

On the walls of our dining room we exhibit and sell the work of a talented local artist, a woman whose vision honestly reflects the beauty of the area in which we live.

Scotty Mitchell came to Boulder in 1998 from the island of Crete, where she and her British husband, Tim, had lived for about twenty years. After just a few short visits, they became so captivated by southern Utah that they "leapt into the unknown" and moved here. "We just fell in love with Boulder," she says. "Having met a few people, we realized it was a varied population—there was a lot more happening than one might expect to find in a small, rural town."

"A lot happening" isn't a phrase commonly heard in reference to the town of Boulder, but for Scotty it meant something different: a change of scenery, quite literally, and the inspiration to move in new directions with her art. Scotty is a plein-air artist. Working on site, she explains, provides an edge of immediacy that breathes vitality into the work; there's a bonding of the artist to the subject. In Greece, she'd painted primarily in oils—Greek gardens, interiors, and scenes from the small, cultivated island of Crete. She now uses mostly pastels to capture southern Utah's dramatic and diverse landscape—the canyons, creeks, hills, mountains, deserts, cliffs, pastures, and massive rock formations—in realistic pinks and purples and greens and blues. "The incredible variety of form and color and the immense scale Utah offers have been a joyous inspiration," she says. "There are different marvels in each direction."

Scotty and Tim were the first to welcome us to Boulder, cooking great meals and sharing their wine with us. "Scotty's blend of Berkeley earthiness and Greek warmth makes her a natural hostess," Jen says. "Everyone feels like they've come home. She has this wonderful, open laugh and a really inclusive way about her."

"I remember how pleased we were when Blake and Jen moved here," says Scotty. "It was winter, and we met at the post office. In a town this size, the post office is where you meet new people—it's the center of our winter social life. It was fun to think that some people wanted to make the grill a nice place. And it's my best venue in Boulder now. I just think the restaurant has become a lovely addition to Boulder. It's a functioning part of the social fabric of town."

Zuni Sweet Potato Skillet Cakes

This is a great accompaniment for grilled meat or delicious served on its own as an appetizer.

    3 pounds sweet potatoes (or yams)
    ½ cup hot water
    ½ cup warmed honey
    1 cup yellow cornmeal
    ½ teaspoon salt

1. Bake sweet potatoes 1 hour at 335 degrees until soft. Let cool about 20 minutes.

2. Squeeze potatoes out of their skins into a medium-sized mixing bowl. Add hot water, honey, cornmeal, and salt, mashing with a fork to combine.

3. Heat 1" canola oil in an 8" cast-iron skillet over medium-high heat till almost smoking. Form a golf-ball-sized blob (a small ice cream scoop works well for this), dip both sides in cornmeal, and flatten slightly into a patty.

5. Fry 3 cakes at a time, 3 minutes on the first side, till edges are firm. Flip and fry another minute till each cake is golden and crispy. Drain on paper towels.

The Bliss of Lists

*Do something every day that you don't want to do; this is the golden rule
for acquiring the habit of doing your duty without pain.*

—MARK TWAIN

We are inveterate list makers—we make lists, we make sublists, we make sub-sublists. And if it weren't a glaring symptom of late-stage psychosis, we might make lists of lists to write.

We post the lists of things we need to do in the kitchen—especially in the case of prepwork—so the items can be publicly crossed off. That way we eliminate the risk of overlapping. There's nothing more frustrating than spending an hour making Pueblo rice pilaf only to discover your business partner has already spent an hour earlier that day making Pueblo rice pilaf. All it leaves you with is an extra batch of Pueblo rice pilaf, one less hour of life to spend with your dog that's needed to go on a run for three days, and a very strong desire to kick someone. We're unashamed to admit that we both also belong to that fine, neurotic species of humans who add to lists the tasks they've already completed, for the bliss that accompanies immediately crossing them off.

We like our list fixation. For Blake, lists serve as natural, noningestible sleeping pills. Unless she writes a list of what needs to be accomplished the following day before going to bed at night, that list gets written inside her mind over and over while she lies in bed attempting to sleep. So it's become not only a daily ritual for her but a nighttime one as well. Our opinion is that you need somewhat of a list brain to run a restaurant or you're probably just not hardwired to make it. We love and believe in the power of lists so completely that we assume everyone feels the same way; hence, we plaster them all over the kitchen—sidework lists, prep lists, what to compost, what not to compost, which drinks to put in which glasses, secrets to dishwashing excellence. We post them assertively, and then, if anything ends up sounding excessively strict or critical, an hour later one of us sneaks back and draws cheerful hearts all over it.

Not surprisingly, this book was also conceived on a bed of lists. One such list was of proposed book titles, some of which, we have been told, are amusing only to us.

List of Rejected Book Titles

Blake and Jen Go to Hell

Go to Hell, Blake and Jen

True Tales from Hell's Backroom

Helen Highwater's

Heck's Backbone Grill

Hell's Belles

Secrets of Skinny Chefs

Hell's Backbone Girls

What If We Threw a Restaurant and Nobody Came?

Kinda Like a Five-Year River Trip

The Mormon the Merrier

Mormon Fuzzy

With a Spoonful of Sugar and a Grain of Salt

A Two-Woman Business in a One-Hundred Horse Town

The Benevolent Dictatorship and How It Worked for Us

Piñon Caramel Sticky Bunz

Our favorite holiday treat, these sticky bunz are sugar-shockingly addictive. The butter kneaded into the dough adds a bakery-pastry quality, and the 2-plus hours of rising time illustrate why bakers work the early morning shifts.

Dough

2¼ teaspoons yeast (1 envelope)
¾ cup warm water (110 degrees)
¼ cup half & half or milk
2 teaspoons vanilla extract
¼ cup sugar
1½ teaspoons baking powder
1 teaspoon salt
1 large egg
4 cups white flour
¼ pound butter (1 stick), slightly softened

Filling

2 tablespoons soft butter
½ cup brown sugar plus 1 tablespoon
  cinnamon, mixed together
1 cup toasted piñons (pine nuts), roughly
  chopped

Caramel

¼ pound butter (1 stick)
½ cup brown sugar
⅓ cup white sugar
½ cup light corn syrup
¼ teaspoon salt
1 cup whole toasted piñons (pine nuts)

1. **Dough:** Stir together yeast, water, and half & half or milk. Let activate for 5 minutes. Combine yeast mixture with all the ingredients except butter to form a soft dough. Knead dough by hand till smooth and supple, about 8 minutes. Knead in the softened butter, a third at a time, until fully incorporated. Place dough in a greased bowl, turn to coat, cover with a damp cloth, and let rise in a warm, draft-free place for 1½ hours or until doubled in bulk.

2. **Shaping and Filling:** Turn dough out onto a lightly floured counter and roll into a rectangle approximately 16 x 12". Dot the soft butter over dough and sprinkle with cinnamon sugar and chopped nuts. Starting at the top left corner, roll dough toward you, forming a nice log. Slice log into 12 pieces. (Cut log in half, cut each half in half, cut each section into thirds.)

3. **Caramel:** Melt all ingredients except toasted piñons in a small pan on the stove. Pour mixture into a greased 9 x 12" casserole pan, making sure the entire bottom is covered with caramel, and sprinkle with 1 cup whole piñons. Place bunz in the prepared pan, cut side down, fitting all 12 in evenly. Cover with lightly greased plastic wrap and allow bunz to double in bulk, about 1 hour.

4. **Baking:** Bake sticky bunz in a preheated 375-degree oven for 17 minutes on the middle rack. Cover with foil and bake another 10 minutes, until light golden brown and bubbling. Remove pan from oven, wait no more than 1 minute, and using oven mitts invert onto serving tray, scraping any sticky goo left behind onto bunz. Beware! If you try to eat the caramel at this point, it will burn the Helen Highwater off your tongue.

Boulder Outdoor Survival School

Before enlightenment—chop wood, carry water.
After enlightenment—chop wood, carry water.

—ZEN BUDDHIST PROVERB

One thing people sometimes notice about Boulder—besides the insanely beautiful, imposing rock formations, the cows and horses, the tranquility and quiet—is the fact that the occasional Boulder resident can be seen walking down the road barefoot, wearing nothing but buckskin, carrying a homemade bow and arrows. These are our friends, the Boulder Outdoor Survival School (BOSS) instructors.

BOSS is an organization that draws people from all over the world to Boulder, where they're trained to survive alone in the wilderness. BOSS's mission is to teach people how to do more with less, to depend on what they know rather than what they're carrying, to accept the heritage of traditional cultures, and to "travel lightly, walk gently, and listen carefully." BOSS offers a variety of courses, each with a different emphasis. On the field course, students and guides hike canyons and mesa tops on trips lasting from four to twenty-eight days, at first carrying virtually nothing—no tents, sleeping bags, water, food, or matches. After completing this first phase of the course, they're typically given a blanket, a poncho, a knife, a compass, some additional clothing, and a water bottle or two. They catch fish, eat cattails, and learn primitive skills, such as how to locate water, build shelter from leaves or snow, and make fire from sticks.

The role of BOSS in our Boulder experience has been significant, for it has introduced a clan of important people into our lives—wise and generous people who continually share with us their knowledge of native skills and ancient practices, and who inspire a very different way of living, viewing the world, and treating the earth.

BOSS instructor Cat Bigney tends a fire to keep the chill off.

Baby's Got the Blues Fudge Brownies

These are what Blake makes when Jen needs a little cheering up. They're amazing alone or with ice cream and a bit of fudge sauce on top. In the name of resourcefulness, we've also taken an overcooked batch and ground them up in the food processor for another terrific ice cream topping.

4 ounces (4 squares) unsweetened chocolate
8 tablespoons (one stick) butter
2 teaspoons vanilla extract
1¼ cups sugar
2 eggs
½ teaspoon salt
½ cup flour

1. Preheat oven to 350 degrees. Grease and flour an 8 x 8" pan.

2. Melt chocolate and butter in a heavy-bottomed saucepan over low heat, stirring continuously until the mixture is smooth.

3. Remove pan from heat and set aside to cool.

4. Add vanilla, sugar, eggs, and salt to the chocolate mixture and beat until thoroughly combined. Add flour and stir until completely mixed.

5. Scrape batter into prepared pan.

6. Bake brownies for about 40 minutes, until top is dry and a straw inserted comes out just barely clean. It's important not to overcook these brownies, so pay attention. (Otherwise you can turn them into a crumb topping!)

7. Let cool in pan on a rack and then cut into squares.

Trash Talking

Nothing in nature is exhausted in its first use. When a thing has served an end to the uttermost, it is wholly new for an ulterior service. In God, every end is converted into new means.

—RALPH WALDO EMERSON

As former backcountry and river chefs, we're conversant with the challenges of trying to integrate environmentally sound practices with business in a locale with inherent obstacles. It can be a struggle even in cities and towns that provide curbside trash and recycling pickup. On the river, what you bring in returns with you when you leave. That means you don't bury your banana peels, leftover sandwiches, or human waste—you pack it up, and it accompanies you on the raft for the remainder of your journey. It offers, in a sense, a good model for living: take responsibility for the garbage you make, and if you don't want to take much responsibility, don't create much garbage.

Our experiences living so closely with nature (and with our trash) have given us the opportunity to see, firsthand, the value of recycling and reusing. Our aim is to be a restaurant with a conscience, and in Boulder this is a view more or less collectively saluted. Boulder's an incredibly forward-thinking town—ordinances and zoning laws are just inclusive enough to grow the town little by little, but exclusive enough to prevent it from becoming a clone of every other town in America with a proliferation of fast-food and motel chains. One ordinance states that sure, there can be a drive-through in Boulder, no problem—with several conditions, including one prohibiting any employee of the drive-through from ever wearing a uniform. And one zoning law stipulates that no new houses that can be seen from the mesa top are allowed to be built. It stands to reason that a town this progressive would offer recycling programs, but due to the remoteness of Boulder, the truth is quite the opposite.

This is another instance of things happening last in our town—no recycling program exists here or in any neighboring towns, for that matter. As a result, we've been forced to rig together an intricate, creative program of our very own. It involves packing garbage bags of aluminum into the car every time we go to a city, collecting our bottles for a local winemaker, and composting our food scraps to fertilize our gardens or feed to some fortunate chickens and dogs. In a town that provides nothing in the way of recycling, it's essential to close the loop of waste by minimizing it from the beginning. We try to make choices and business decisions—from purchasing to trash disposal—that are thoughtful and responsible. We buy recycled products; all our paper products are made from 100 percent post-consumer waste. We never buy or store food in single-serve, disposable portions. Breakfast jam and butter are spooned into cruets, and we use cloth napkins instead of paper (with no laundry service in town, we don't have dry-cleaning chemicals on our conscience either—we just spray the heck out of the napkins every night with a stain remover, machine-wash them, and hope for the best). And our tables with their galvanized metal tops are gorgeous, but this is no accident—they're beautiful so as to eliminate the need for tablecloths.

Because Boulder has no curbside garbage pickup either, each day we tranport the restaurant trash in our cars to one of fifteen public dumpsters in town. The dumpsters are emptied only once a week; this shortage of trash receptacles rules out wastefulness. Because our waste-disposal system demands such unremitting discipline and organization on the part of everyone at the grill, we put a great deal of thought into managing our trash. We constantly dig through restaurant garbage to find compostable vegetable ends and to pull out cans. This makes it easier to face ourselves in the mirror, knowing that we're letting our Green flag fly, but it shatters any illusion we might cling to of being glamorous restaurateurs.

It is not, by any stretch of the imagination, a simple task to run an environmentally sound business in our little bucolic heaven, but our rule is no haphazard decisions—everything we grow, buy, and order must be used and used and used and reused. It can be an inconvenience, but just as when we run out of food, it also presents an opportunity to tell customers about the unique nature of our remote restaurant: Sorry, there's no beef tonight because we used up the whole cow already. Sorry, we don't serve any bottled beer because we can't recycle the glass. They may grumble at the time, but ultimately the situation offers them a deeper understanding of the value of reducing and might even reframe their experience of recycling and the true costs of consumption.

Gloria's pig, Rosie, eagerly awaits the bucket of restaurant kitchen scraps that we faithfully save for her.

Our Beloved Colleen

*I tell you, the more I think, the more I feel that
there is nothing more truly artistic than to love people.*

—VINCENT VAN GOGH

She writes love letters to people at work when she thinks they need a pick-me-up or to tell them they're doing a good job, and when she does the cooking at night, she leaves a "good morning" or "have a great day" note on the line for the breakfast cook. When we're sick, she brings us Mason jars of homemade chicken noodle soup. She lends us videos from her massive collection free of charge (this is huge, considering the profit she could turn in a town with no video store). She's our friend, unfailing ally, nurturer, on-site therapist, and assistant manager. We may provide the Hell and Grill in this restaurant, but Colleen Thompson is our Backbone.

It's not just that Colleen is hardworking and efficient—it's that she's the sole employee at the grill who's mastered the unenviable job of being both of us at the same time. Because she understands the nuances of our two divergent but symbiotic work roles (back of house, front of house), she has the knowledge and ability to help us in ways we don't even know how to help each other. Colleen's a textbook Libra: straightforward, introspective, wonderfully opinionated, and fiercely loyal. She's simultaneously wise, supportive, and open-minded and the first person we trusted enough to babysit our little labor of love, Helles. Our lives are absurd and exhausting, but without Colleen they'd be unmanageable. Occasionally, when one of us is approaching final burnout, she senses it, steps in, and executes an act no other employee could ever really do—she tells us to go home. At which point we make fluttering, throaty noises of gratitude and scurry off to our cars as fast as we can.

Colleen has lived in Boulder since 1994 and worked at all three restaurants in town. A mother of four, she's been in and out of the restaurant business since she was fifteen years old. Initially, she came to us looking for a second, part-time job—something to keep her occupied during the summers when she wasn't cooking lunches for the elementary school kids of Boulder. She'd been preparing the lunches for six years, but eventually she quit the school and is now with us full-time. "It was hard stepping into a new position," Colleen says, "but I'm really happy. I made the right decision. These guys treat me great, and when someone treats you that well, it's easy to reciprocate."

Well-respected in the LDS community but no longer practicing, Colleen is a never-ending source of knowledge about the church and seems to act as a liaison of sorts between the two communities. "I believe all things are possible," she says. "That's why things work so well up here. There's Blake and Jen, the town and the Buddhism, ranchers, environmentalists, people who want growth and who don't, and all those in between. It gives me a lot to think about.

"I'm here at the grill full-time because I believe in the girls' vision 100 percent, wholeheartedly," Colleen says. "I love the way they try to bring in all different kinds of organic foods. They live the whole experience of it—not just the food, but the entire vision. They actually live what they believe, to the best of their ability, and they bring that to the restaurant—they bring that to us. It's a constant, daily thing, even with the stress—people don't understand what a stressful business this is. I think, 'Why didn't they break a long time ago?' and they're not going to—it's the love and compassion along with the professional approach. Blake and Jen can be upset with each other, sit down at a table, and within a few minutes it's all over—they're laughing. It's such a together thing."

Early March

I need more grace than I thought.

—RUMI

The days become incrementally warmer, and before we know it our long winter respite begins rolling up like a rug under our feet. We cling desperately to the final days of leisurely meals and uninterrupted sleep, but alas, it's in vain, because the guests are back, peering hopefully through the dust on the restaurant windows, phoning in reservations. Leaving long messages.

We can hide from them no longer.

It's time to unlock our doors to a new season and all that comes with it; time to work again, feed and serve. Time to remember that cooking is an art and a gift—and as a career, an incredible privilege.

A Debt of Gratitude

We are deeply thankful to everyone who provided the love, support, and skill that led to the success of our restaurant and the completion of this book: first and foremost, the brilliantly talented Eric Swanson, for getting us into this beautiful mess and skillfully guiding the boat, and the beyond amazing Maria Levy, for the vision to see it and the talent to create it. To the sublime Lavinia Spalding for everything, everything, everything; our mothers for bringing us into this world: Dolly Spalding, editor, proofreader, recipe tester, and head cheerleader, and Maria Michnovicz for her everlasting faith and confidence; his emminence Chagdud Tulku Rinpoche; Terry Tempest Williams for understanding us; Brooke Williams for encouraging us; Lama Shenpen Drolma for her precise edits, spiritual advice, and kindness in allowing us to excerpt from her book; thanks to Renny Levy for being rock solid; our attorneys, Good Prince Shawn Ferrin and Jack Sullivan; to Sara Stathas, photo assistant, hostess with the mostess, and darn good company. Thanks to Virginia Rainey, Rebecca Chastenet de Géry; to Sur La Table, which supplied the prettiest-ever dishes for our photo shoot; Susan Massey, food stylist extraordinaire, for her patience and brilliant sense of humor; to Thérèse Shere and Peg Goldstein for cleaning up our mess. We are indebted to Lulu Santamaria and Patrice Horstman for showing up just in time; to Curtis and Diane Oberhansly; Bill and Cheryl Jamison for inspiration and counsel; John Vlahides for urging us to keep it real and ending this project on a high note; to Heather Plumb for her hard work. And a million thanks to all our recipe testers: Bonnie Ulmer, Birgit Buss, Nancy Chabott, Martha Shimano, Debbie Hearn, Keith Todhunter, Nicole Wesley, and Veronica Voss.

This book would never have crystallized into existence without the grill, and the grill wouldn't be here without everyone who gave generously of their time, hearts, minds, or muscles. Love and eternal gratitude, above all, to Stuart Henderson, who helped us birth little baby Helles, and Uncle Mark "Moky" Michnovicz, Helles's first nanny. Great appreciation goes to everyone not already mentioned in the book who has, in working for or with us, made the grill a special place: Debi Stout, Deborah Hughes, James O'Day, Joe Parker, Bryce and Jessica, Mike Nelson, Lara McKerracher, Brynn, Scott, and Larkin Brodie, Paulette Ksiesak, Jeff Sanders, the Heaton family, Eddie Young, and Gwendolyn Zeta. A bazillion thanks to the staff of our 2004 season for giving so much and affording us the space to finish this project; Stacy and Jennifer Davis for sticking with us from the beginning; Ana Rendón, the brave and the beautiful; Sara Zorzakis, yo sister, soul sister; Vlasto Slovak for pulling off the greatest rescue of all time; Paxton Bigler, Chester Fantastic, Shannon, Addie, and Jack. Enormous thank-you hugs to our army of peerless friends who came to visit and doubled as waitstaff, especially Amy Flynn, Emma Gardner, Dee Ann Tracy, Anne Doyle, Julia McCullough; Sheila Smith, who cleaned us up so right; Shadrup and Lara, who provided a beautiful dharma infusion and kept our bellies happy and full; Jeremy and Michelle, Nathanael and Chanda Spalding; Trish Hawkins, a true-blue friend; Sam Jones for making the world a more beautiful place; Jabe Beal; Marie Trunnell (Frenchy! Come back for a dance!); Sean Harris; Matt Graham, glad we keep finding each other; Becky Vollenweider, Sinuhe and Steph, Gloria's clan, and Eric and Mary Feiler.

Everlasting thank-yous to all the friends and fans of the grill: Stephanie McCarthy, who created a more beautiful us; Martha Clark and Thad Stewart, Mary and Gary Garland; Doctor BJ Miller—you won all our hearts; Scott, Barbara, and Dane Berry, Josh Bernstein and the staff at BOSS, Mary Malouf. Thanks to all our Hell's Backbone girls and boys for keeping us young: Anna Swanson, Pearl Protiva-Spear, Emma Cole Hart, Mandy Callaham, Chloe Jones, Nico and Dakota Swanson, and Jake and Evan Levy; Mayor Gailey, Farlon Buhanin, and all the town council, Bill and Adalee Muse, Peggy and Jack Carroll, Dennis Bertucci, Wulf, Kristen and Trina Barsch, Ashley Coombs, Martina and Anselm, Camille Ballard, Jan Belknap, Sherry and Gary Catmull, Candace and Cory, Gary Pankow, Robert and Donna Owen; Holly Hopper, all-star customer and friend supreme, Dixie at Stone Canyon Inn; Michelle and Joe from the Mean Bean in Springdale; the Drepung Loseling Monastery; Ken Kraus; Bruce Fulmer and the Garfield Travel Council; Barbara Love and John Bryant, the folks at DABC; our suppliers and our random repairers of things; Kenny McCoy for all he does and tries; Mike Garrity; the people of SUWA who work tirelessly to preserve this beautiful place that inspires all our efforts; Western Spirit Cycling for loving us even though we don't actually ride bikes; all the journalists—thank you doesn't even scratch the surface; Murray Hidary and Jimmy Demers—a bowl of soup + a tumble into the pond = friends forever.

We cannot begin to express our gratitude to: Susie Protiva, who feng shui'd us into a new economic bracket and is the finest friend; Bret Benge and Rajean Bifano, who keep us looking so damn good; Kurt Brungardt, who has been such a significant friend; Raymond Shurtz; Nathan Jones, who has always cheered us on and talked us down; Ian Vollmer; the ever-sweet Kate and Jack Sullivan, dearest Willow, Nicole, Tonya, and Lainie for the lifelines; Mark Piller for the challenge; Jack and Susan Pollack, Sandra and Howard Miller, Anne Gwinn, Graydon Briggs, Shane and Robin Robison, Lynn and Paul Bown, and Jeanne Aldrich.

Extra-special thanks go to the ever-generous and benevolent Dave Mock; the wise and venerable Cindy Shumway; Khentrul Lodro Thaye Rinpoche, Lama Drimed; Oprah Winfrey and *O the Oprah* magazine for the golden doorway; Gretchen Reynolds, Mindy Sink; Steve Glazer for never-ending guidance and goodness; the Michnovicz family; the Spalding and Blodgett families, especially Blake's late father, Walter, for his promotion and encouragement; Bonnie Swanson and the Swanson clan; superpower friend Blaire Kribs; Tim Macy for demonstrating a model for a business based on personal ethics; Kelly Poe Wilson for teaching so much, up to and including the all-important "accept the mess" mantra; Becky Moore McKay for unwavering love, support, and friendship; kisses and hugs to Patty Moore and Aunt Sue for their exuberant enthusiasm and to the Stemmlers for their nurturing. Thanks to each person who drove so far to reach us and to those who keep coming back; the body-workers, wine-bringers, and grocery-getters; those who danced and hula-hooped with us; those who paved the way before us.

Lavinia would like to thank all her beloved friends who encouraged her and understood when she wouldn't answer her phone for eight months (especially Erin, Lynn, Kim, Amy, and Scotty); Erica Hilton, who provided insightful comments, red wine, Ben and Jerry's, a personal airport shuttle service, and countless late-night pep talks; Jeremy Burnett, who gave invaluable early-stage suggestions; and Anthony Weller, her fairy godfather of writing, for his boundless generosity, honest and precise skill, and enduring belief in her.

And lastly, unending gratitude to all of our wonderful friends, neighbors, and business associates who agreed to be interviewed, photographed, and profiled for this book, those who listened and gave advice—gave all they had. We bow down before anyone and everyone who has helped us become more loving, more compassionate, more sane, and more open. Double-plus thank-you.

Resources

Anasazi State Park Museum contains an ancient village that was one of the largest ancestral Puebloan communities west of the Colorado River. Archaeological excavations at the site have revealed more than one hundred structures and have produced thousands of artifacts, some of which are on display in the museum exhibit halls.

Winter hours: 9–5
Summer hours: 8–6
435-335-7308
www.stateparks.utah.gov

Boulder Mountain Fly Fishing offers guided fly-fishing trips on Boulder Mountain. Lessons and equipment provided. Call for reservations.

435-335-7306
E-mail: stevestoner@direcway.com
www.bouldermountainflyfishing.com

Since 1968, the **Boulder Outdoor Survival School** (BOSS) has offered people the opportunity to explore the wilderness without a dependence on modern technology and gear. BOSS emphasizes traditional techniques, teaching the art of low-tech travel and the primitive skills of indigenous cultures.

800-335-7404
www.boss-inc.com

The **Burr Trail Outpost** is an eclectic shop and espresso bar featuring the works of local artists, as well as gifts, jewelry, outdoor gear, books, and maps. Located on the corner of the Burr Trail and Highway 12.

Open March through October: 8:30–6
435-335-7565
www.burrtrailoutpost.com

At **Hell's Backbone Ranch & Trails** you can ride well-mannered, happy horses over slickrock trails, red canyons, and aspen meadows. No experience necessary. Two-hour to multiday/drop camps. Contact Breck and Becky Crystal.

435-335-7581
www.bouldermountaintrails.com or
breckcrystal@yahoo.com

Since 1991, **Escalante Canyon Outfitters** has offered hiking trips into the canyons of southern Utah from their base in Boulder, Utah. Each trip includes four to nine people and offers everything you'd expect from a first-class wilderness adventure, plus horses to carry the gear. Days are spent exploring the Escalante and evenings relaxing in camp with good company and excellent meals.

888-326-4453
435-335-7499 fax
www.ecohike.com

Boulder Exchange is a country-style grocery in a historic Boulder building with sundries, fishing supplies, ice, and 24/7 pay-at-the-pump gas and diesel. RV parking with hookups is available. Located on Highway 12, next door to the Anasazi State Park.

435-335-7304

Hills & Hollows is a friendly convenience store featuring organic and natural foods, T-shirts, unique gifts, maps, and camping supplies, with 24/7 pay-at-the-pump gas and diesel. On the hill—west of Highway 12.

www.hillshollows.com

Pole's Place Gift Shop offers souvenirs, books, pottery, jewelry, T-shirts, and locally crafted quilts, rugs, and handmade gifts. Located across the street from the Anasazi State Park on Highway 12.

435-335-7422
www.boulderutah.com/polesplace

Red Rock 'n' Llamas offers guided llama support trips in the Grand Staircase-Escalante National Monument, Glen Canyon National Recreation Area, and Rainbow Bridge National Monument.

877-9LLAMAS
www.redrocknllamas.com

Wolf Hollow Outfitters and Saddlery specializes in backcountry guiding, catering to photographers, wildlife viewers, and traditional hunters, and produces custom leather cowboy gear and saddles. Contact Aram Barsch.

435-335-7455
www.wolfhollowoutfitters.com
E-mail: wolfhollowoutfitters@yahoo.com

Additional Resources

Hell's Backbone Grill
P.O. Box 1421, #20 North Highway 12
Boulder, UT 84716
435-335-7464
www.hellsbackbonegrill.com

Boulder Mountain Lodge
P.O. Box 1397, #20 North Highway 12
Boulder, UT 84716
800-556-3446
435-335-7460
www.boulder-utah.com

Native Seeds/SEARCH
3061 North Campbell Ave., Tucson, AZ 85719
520-622-5561
www.nativeseeds.org

For information on the Buddhist teachings of Chagdud Tulku Rinpoche and the meditation centers he established:

Rigdzin Ling
P.O. Box 279, Junction City, CA 96048
530-623-2714
info@chagdudgonpa.org
www.chagdudgonpa.org

For information on Boddhisattva Peace Trainings and the book *Change of Heart*:

Iron Knot Ranch
Lama Shenpen Drolma
P.O. Box 769, Silver City, NM 88062
510-315-1960
www.ironknot.org

Selected Bibliography

The following texts were consulted during the writing of this book. The indirect and invaluable guidance of the authors listed is recognized and sincerely appreciated.

Chesher, Greer K. *Heart of the Desert Wild.* Bryce Canyon National Park, UT: Bryce Canyon National History Association, 2000.

Cooks Illustrated magazine. *The Best Recipe.* Brookline, MA: 1999.

Corriher, Shirley O. *CookWise: The Hows and Whys of Successful Cooking.* New York: William Morrow and Co, Inc. 1997.

Cunningham, Marion. *The Fannie Farmer Baking Book.* New York: Alfred A. Knopf, 1984.

Drolma, Lama Shenpen, ed. *Change of Heart: The Bodhisattva Peace Training of Chagdud Tulku.* Junction City, CA: Padma Publishing, 2004.

Jamison, Bill, and Cheryl Alters. *American Home Cooking*. New York: Broadway, 1999.

LeFevre, Lenora. *Boulder Country and Its People.* Springville, UT: Art City Publishing, 1973.

Lukins, Sheila, and Julie Rosso. *The Silver Palate Cookbook.* New York: Workman Publishing, 1979.

Madison, Deborah. *Vegetarian Cooking for Everyone.* New York: Broadway, 1997.

Moosewood Collective. *Moosewood Restaurant Book of Desserts.* New York: Clarkson Potter, 1997.

Moosewood Collective. *New Recipes from Moosewood Restaurant.* Berkeley, CA: Ten Speed Press, 1987.

Ostling, Richard N. and Joan K. *Mormon America: The Power and the Promise.* San Francisco: Harper, 1999.

Rombauer, Irma S., Marion Rombauer, and Ethan Becker. *The New All-Purpose Joy of Cooking.* New York: Scribner, 1997.

Scoble, Gretchen, and Ann Field. *The Meaning of Flowers.* San Francisco: Chronicle Books, 1998.

Spears, Grady. *A Cowboy in the Kitchen.* Berkeley, CA: Ten Speed Press, 1998.

Index

The photographs in this book were all produced digitally using the following equipment and software: Canon EOS 1Ds camera, Canon lenses, iView editing software, Phase One C1 Pro image processing software, Adobe Photoshop, Image Print RIP for proofing on a Epson 7600 printer, Apple G4 notebook and desktop computers, La Cie hard drives, and a Sony Artisan monitor. I would like to thank the following people for their help: James Bourland of Borderline Press; Sara Stathas; Maggie Blanchard; Sarah Stewart Auman of Showcase Photographics in Atlanta, GA; Julieanne Kost of Adobe Software; Scott Erickson and Martin Skrzypczak of Digital Technology Group in Tampa, FL; and Vicki McDermott of Camera and Darkroom in Santa Fe, NM.

PROVECHO PRESS
is a partnership between a designer
and a photographer. Our goal is
to create beautiful, independent,
thought-provoking books.
www.provechopress.com